WORCESTER
LOCOMOTIVE SHED

WORCESTER LOCOMOTIVE SHED

ENGINES AND TRAIN WORKINGS

Steve Bartlett

PEN & SWORD
TRANSPORT

AN IMPRINT OF PEN & SWORD BOOKS LTD.
YORKSHIRE – PHILADELPHIA

Dedication

To Worcester's shed staff and footplate crews, who worked in difficult and sometimes challenging times in a rapidly changing industry.

First published in Great Britain in 2020 by
Pen and Sword Transport

An imprint of Pen & Sword Books Ltd
Yorkshire - Philadelphia

Copyright © Steve Bartlett, 2020

ISBN: 978 1 52675 059 4

Typeset by Aura Technology and Software Services, India.
Printed and bound by Printworks Global Ltd, London/Hong Kong.

Pen & Sword Books Ltd incorporates the Imprints of Pen & Sword Books Archaeology, Atlas, Aviation, Battleground, Discovery, Family History, History, Maritime, Military, Naval, Politics, Railways, Select, Transport, True Crime, Fiction, Frontline Books, Leo Cooper, Praetorian Press, Seaforth Publishing, Wharncliffe and White Owl.

For a complete list of Pen & Sword titles please contact
PEN & SWORD BOOKS LIMITED
47 Church Street, Barnsley, South Yorkshire, S70 2AS, England
E-mail: enquiries@pen-and-sword.co.uk
Website: www.pen-and-sword.co.uk

or

PEN AND SWORD BOOKS
1950 Lawrence Rd, Havertown, PA 19083, USA
E-mail: Uspen-and-sword@casematepublishers.com
Website: www.penandswordbooks.com

Contents

Acknowledgements

This work has been built around personal records and memories of the Worcester railway scene in the 1960s, supplemented by latter day research, including the railway records at the National Archives Kew. To this has been added the personal contributions of former Worcester footplate and shed staff, who lived through the times and events described. In particular my thanks go to the Worcester Locomotive Society, an active gathering point for Worcester's former railwaymen and like-minded enthusiasts.

My grateful thanks go to those who generously shared their photograph collections to bring this story to life, including Laurence Waters for the Great Western Trust, Paul Shackcloth for the Manchester Locomotive Society, Terry Walsh for the R.G. Nelson collection, Ben Ashworth, John Goss, Robert Pritchard, Andrew Smith, Ron Herbert, Gerald Robinson, Tim Farebrother, Richard Postill, Dave Waldren, Roy Palmer, Nigel Kendall, David Nicholas, Roy Denison, C.M. & J.M. Bentley, Gordon Coltas Trust, Ralph Ward, Roger Lamb, Worcester Locomotive Society for the Fred Cole collection, Ian Catling, John Mudge, Ray Smith for the Terry Rudd collection, Pete Skelton for the Derek Short collection and Chris Wilkinson.

Special thanks go to Anthony Haynes for making available his father F.A. Haynes' very special and largely unpublished Cotswolds route photographs, to Mick Rock for recording his Worcester fireman's memories and Brian Penney for his in depth knowledge of the Running and Maintenance department scene both regionally and at Worcester. Informal photographs of Worcester's shed and footplate staff have sometimes proved difficult to correctly credit as often prints were passed on from original photographers through several pairs of hands. These images add an important human element to a story that could easily have just been about machines and events. Also acknowledgement goes to the several photographic libraries that filled essential gaps to complete the story; their photographs individually credited.

I am particularly grateful to Richard Soddy for his excellent work drafting the shed plans and maps throughout the book.

Finally thanks to my wife Lin who lived through the many weeks and months spent bringing this saga together. My apologies if any names have been omitted or photographs incorrectly credited. Everything possible has been done to check and acknowledge original sources.

WORCESTER AREA MAP

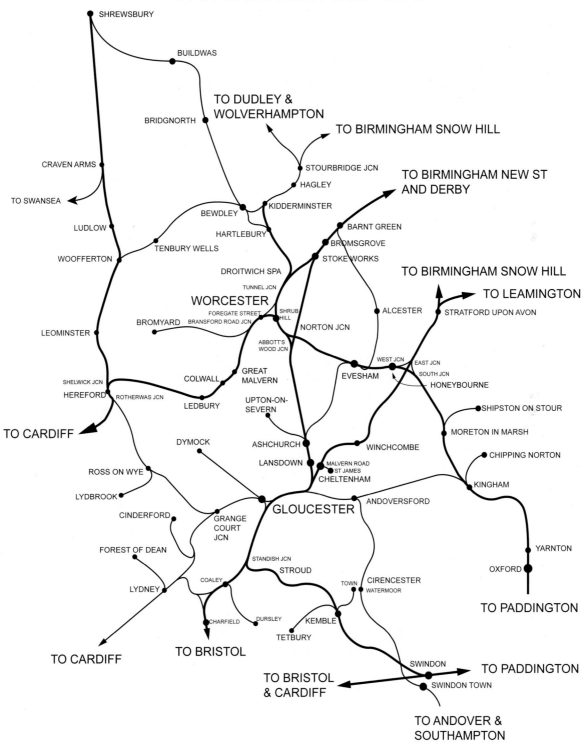

DRAWING - R.SODDY

Introduction

Boughton Halt was located one and a half miles west of Worcester Foregate Street station on the line to Hereford. Opened in March 1924, it had an infrequent service and was the location for my earliest railway memories, watching trains after primary school. Here an ex-GWR 4MT 2-6-2T runs into the unkempt halt with a local passenger service. M. HALE. GREAT WESTERN TRUST

My earliest memories of Worcester go back to the 1950s, when at six years of age and after school my mother would walk me and my younger sister in her pushchair along the footpath to Boughton Halt on the railway approaches to Worcester from Hereford. There, to coin a time honoured phrase, we would sit and watch the trains although none ever seemed to stop there. In the school holidays, we would venture further to the next minor station Rushwick Halt. I recall there in the season that hop pickers on their annual pilgrimage from the West Midlands could be seen working in the hop field next to the railway. It would be at this time that my lifelong fascination with railways would start. Services passing by might be a gleaming Worcester or Old Oak Common 'Castle' locomotive racing through on a Paddington to Hereford express or a sleek but almost silent ex-Great Western Railway diesel railcar, gliding through on a local passenger service to Malvern or Bromyard. The line was also a heavy freight route from South Wales to the West Midlands and a filthy freight locomotive might next slog past with a long noisy goods train.

The family had recently moved to Worcester when my father George Bartlett, a third generation railwayman and GWR trained Swindon Works mechanical engineer, had become Worcester's Assistant District Motive Power Superintendent in October 1954. He had previously been a comparatively young shed master at Swansea Paxton Street and briefly so at Shrewsbury. A few years later, we would move on to South Wales where he took a similar job in the larger Neath Motive Power District. However, he, with the family, would return in January 1960 to the top

Rushwick Halt, next down the line from Boughton Halt and also opened in March 1924. Here was where I ventured further afield with the family at six years of age to pursue the time honoured tradition of watching the trains. ANDREW SMITH COLLECTION

job of Running and Maintenance Officer Gloucester. This was in effect the former Worcester District managed from a new location, although the traditional shed code hierarchy of 85A Worcester and 85B Gloucester Horton Road would remain unchanged. My father never lost that close affinity with Worcester and an early 1960s group photo shows him awarding a sports trophy to Worcester staff. Just a few of his personal records have survived and will be used as this story unfolds alongside other surviving records from the time.

As I entered my teenage years, I inevitably succumbed to becoming a rail enthusiast and later would follow the family tradition becoming a fourth generation railwayman. Ironically, many years later in the privatised railway world, I was responsible for Central Trains' train planning team in Birmingham. Worcester at that time became the preferred depot to concentrate train crew work on passenger services to Cardiff, Nottingham and the Birmingham area, helping to ensure its future in the modern railway world.

However, we must now return to Worcester at the dawn of the 1960s. The city's railway infrastructure was then and indeed still is dominated by the triangle of railway routes to the north of Shrub Hill and Foregate Street stations. Worcester's locomotive shed was located on a comparatively cramped site within the triangle. Whilst this location gave flexibility for depot access and egress, it also constrained expansion of the depot's facilities.

The main line from South Wales via Hereford approached the city through Foregate Street station, then reaching Rainbow Hill Junction at the triangle's western end. The left fork there headed northwards along the side of the triangle to Tunnel Junction and beyond to Kidderminster, Stourbridge Junction and Birmingham Snow Hill. Services

from Hereford for Oxford and London Paddington took the right hand fork at Rainbow Hill Junction, along the second side of the triangle into Shrub Hill station. The third right hand side of the triangle ran north from Shrub Hill towards Tunnel Junction, where it joined the route from Foregate Street to the West Midlands. This third side of the triangle passed the engine shed site on the left and on the right Worcester Works, behind that was the freight yard and goods avoiding line.

The existence of two separate Worcester stations at Foregate Street and Shrub Hill was and is not ideal. Each in fact had sound commercial and operational reasons for their location. Whilst services from Hereford to London Paddington could serve both stations, those from South Wales to Birmingham Snow Hill, after calling at Foregate Street, headed directly north along the left hand side of the triangle. To run these via Shrub Hill required a reversal there and, prior to DMU introduction, an engine change. Routing these services via Shrub Hill also introduced a through journey time penalty. Foregate Street was also the most convenient for the city's shopping centre, but its site was restricted by its elevated position above street level which limited it to basic up and down platforms. Shrub Hill, by contrast, whilst commercially not so well located, had a more generous rail layout and station frontage. It had lengthy up and down through platforms, each with bays to the side. The up platform had a very useful mid-platform crossover leading to the centre through line. The latter allowed mid-platform engine release and most importantly non-passenger traffic to pass through the station unhindered. The engine release facility made it the location of choice for engine changes and portion combining on Hereford-Worcester-Paddington services.

The former Midland Railway main line from Derby and Birmingham New Street to Bristol, with its regular cross country express passenger and freight services, passed by without a second glance at the city some three miles to the east of Worcester. The route's local passenger and some freight services did however run via Worcester, leaving the Midland route at Stoke Works Junction south of Bromsgrove, running into Droitwich Spa and from there to Worcester Shrub Hill. From there, services re-joined the Midland Railway route by dropping down the chord line from Norton Junction to Abbotts Wood Junction. This had given the Midland Railway valuable running rights into and through the otherwise GWR-dominated Worcester area. It also meant that Worcester regularly saw a variety of ex-LMS motive power passing through and also being serviced on shed.

Worcester was also the crossroads for a number of long distance cross

Worcester Shrub Hill on a busy 4 June 1963 afternoon, with Worcester's No 7928 *Wolf Hall* recently arrived on the up platform with a portion from Hereford for Paddington. The points are already set to release the engine through the mid-platform crossover. The fresh Paddington-bound engine at the head of the Worcester starting portion is out of view ahead on the same platform. This will shortly set back and couple up to the Hereford portion. The locomotive shed is in the background, whilst young schoolboys watch the busy scene from the adjoining down platform. NEVILL STEAD COLLECTION. TRANSPORT TREASURY

Shrub Hill Junction with Gloucester Barnwood's BR Standard 5MT 4-6-0 No 73068 departing with the 7.33am Gloucester Eastgate to Birmingham New Street on 30 April 1963. Shrub Hill Junction signal box and the engine shed are in the background. BEN ASHWORTH

Worcester Shed viewed from the Shrub Hill area on 17 April 1964. The Passenger Shed is in the foreground with the Goods Shed behind. A 5MT 'Hall' 4-6-0 and a rare visiting 6MT 'County' 4-6-0 stand prepared for their next duties, whilst three of Worcester's 7P 'Castle' 4-6-0s can be seen withdrawn on the siding beyond. ROY DENISON

Worcester Tunnel Junction lies ahead with the main line north from Shrub Hill heading towards the tunnel in the distance. It's 1 June 1963 and the engines on the left are on the shed coaling road; the photograph taken from that structure. The shunting engine positions locomotive coal wagons containing South Wales steam coal and the universally disliked reformed 'ovoids' whilst a DMU approaches from the Birmingham direction. The single diesel power car is stood where ex-GWR diesel rail cars were once serviced. Worcester Yard and the freight avoiding line lie to the far right. R.C. RILEY. TRANSPORT TREASURY

Worcester Freight Yard forms the backdrop as Newport Ebbw Junction's 8F 2-8-0 No 3807 starts a freight off the Freight Avoiding Line for the West Midlands on 13 June 1964. Tunnel Junction signal box can be seen in the foreground. BEN ASHWORTH

Vinegar Branch flat crossing from left to right passes over the sharply curving side of the Worcester triangle from Shrub Hill in the background to Rainbow Hill Junction, Foregate Street and Hereford. The Vinegar Branch started from the shed site out of view on the left and will on the right drop steeply down over an ungated road crossing to private sidings beyond. TIM FAREBROTHER

country freight routes. This resulted in a much broader range of freight motive power passing through the city than was the case with passenger services. Long distance freight trains used all three sides of the triangle, most pausing to take water and train crew relief at a convenient point. This gave Worcester a large extra footplate commitment relieving these through freight services, most therefore worked by other depots'

through locomotives. However, not forgotten must be the local freight trips that left and returned to Worcester serving local stations in the wider area. It was therefore not surprising that the Great Western Railway established a major motive power depot within the city. All of this made Worcester in the last decade of steam operations a fascinating rail centre to work in and observe.

Worcester Shed Layout and Facilities

WORCESTER SHED

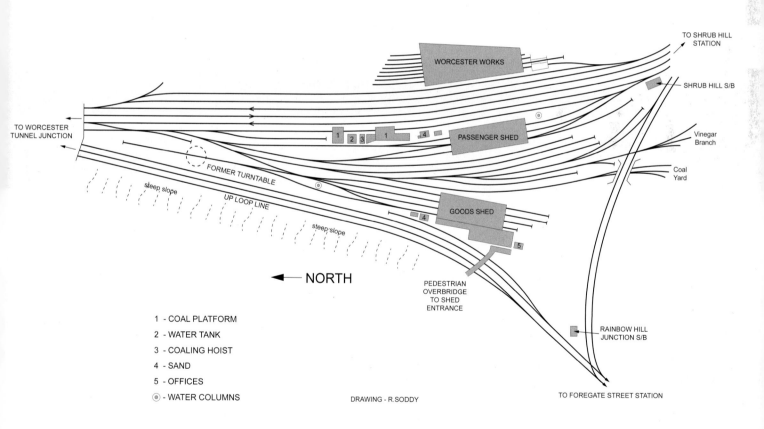

TO SHRUB HILL
STATION

WORCESTER WORKS

SHRUB HILL S/B

TO WORCESTER
TUNNEL JUNCTION

Vinegar
Branch

PASSENGER SHED

Coal
Yard

FORMER TURNTABLE

steep slope

UP LOOP LINE

steep slope

GOODS SHED

◄— NORTH

PEDESTRIAN
OVERBRIDGE
TO SHED
ENTRANCE

RAINBOW HILL
JUNCTION S/B

1 - COAL PLATFORM

2 - WATER TANK

3 - COALING HOIST

4 - SAND

5 - OFFICES

◉ - WATER COLUMNS

DRAWING - R.SODDY

TO FOREGATE STREET STATION

Worcester Shed in an atmospheric panoramic scene in the 1950s. The shed is viewed from the north towards Shrub Hill on the top far left. Individual shed buildings and facilities can be identified by cross-checking with the shed plan. Prominent are the Passenger Shed upper left, the Goods Engine Shed to the right and the rather ungainly looking coal hoist on the extreme left. In the background a Paddington to Hereford service rounds the curve from Shrub Hill to Foregate Street, whilst a selection of mostly local locomotive classes is on view around the shed site. Identifiable centre stage are Worcester's 4MT 2-6-2T No 4571 and Saltley's 4MT 2-6-0 No 43036. M. Hale. Great Western Trust

The city's motive power depot was located within the rail triangle that lay to the north of Foregate Street and Shrub Hill stations. The two main shed buildings dated from 1853 and the Oxford, Worcester and Wolverhampton Railway. In 1860, the latter would merge with others to briefly form the West Midlands Railway, which in 1863 became part of an expanding Great Western Railway. It would remain in this ownership until rail nationalisation in 1948. The two shed buildings were known, a little misleadingly, as the Goods Engine Shed, whose dimensions were 150ft long and 60ft wide, and the Passenger Engine Shed, 152ft long and 50ft wide. The respective titles did not in any way reflect their current practical use. However, the names were in common usage at the depot in the 1960s and however inaccurate were used then and here for identification purposes. The three tracks Passenger Shed was located on the east side of the site nearest to Shrub Hill Junction, with access towards the station. The four roads Goods Shed was on the furthest north-west side of the depot. Both were brick built and originally had slate roofs fitted with smoke ventilators. The roofs had been renewed on a number of occasions and by the 1960s were of overlaid corrugated iron sheeting.

Between the two shed buildings were sidings shared with the traffic department. Several were used for engine stabling and later storage, whilst the traffic sidings were mainly for Vinegar branch traffic and an adjacent coal depot. Within this group of sidings, one track, the previously mentioned Vinegar branch, led via a flat crossing over the main line between Rainbow Hill and Shrub Hill Junctions. It then made a gradual descent over an ungated public road to serve Hill Evans and company, vinegar distillers, as well as Heenan and Froude's engineering company private siding. A second through siding ran between the two sheds in the same area down a steep 1 in 16 gradient, taking it under the main line to Underwood's coal yard and a gas works.

The shed, although having a large tender engine allocation, rather unusually had no turntable. There had once been a small forty-two feet turntable on the siding next to the running line from Rainbow Hill Junction to Tunnel Junction, stop blocked at the Tunnel Junction end. This became disused before the Second World War and the pit filled with locomotive ash. Locomotives were now turned via the triangle surrounding the depot. Although this was a versatile arrangement it could be time consuming and waste line occupation in a busy operational area. There were two access and egress points from the depot; one at the Shrub Hill end of the site leading from the Passenger Shed.

The other was at the northern Tunnel Junction end of the layout. Drivers when 'requesting the road' off shed from the signal box were required to indicate the route around the triangle they wished to take to ensure their engines were facing the right direction for their next train working.

Locomotive preparation had its challenges as Worcester fireman Mick Rock recalls:

'A common problem at many steam depots, including Worcester, was finding tools when preparing a locomotive. Western locos were issued with a complete set when out shopped from Swindon, however even when the tool boxes were provided with new locks they were soon opened. There seemed to be a continual cycle of "rob Peter to pay Paul". The worst involved an engine that had been stopped for repairs or boiler washouts. These would often be found with hardly any tools remaining and the preparing crew would be faced with taking tools from another out of service loco. The list of tools required was a shovel, coal pick, oil feeder, engine oil can, lubricator oil can, flare lamp, gauge glass lamp, bucket, hand brush, detonators and flags, long pricker, short pricker, fire box shovel, fire iron, smoke plate and ring, scanners for piston glands and gauge glass. Finding all these took time and when a crew was only given an hour to fully prepare a loco, time was our greatest enemy. Midland engines visiting Worcester tended to retain all of their tools whilst on shed – very strange.'

The depot's coaling arrangements left much to be desired and were poor in comparison with the large standard coaling stages provided at most ex-GWR main depots. A somewhat primitive crane and bucket loading arrangements had been improved to some extent in 1944 by the installation of an electrically operated Stothert & Pitt coaling hoist. This design is believed to be only found here and at Southall shed. The equipment comprised a mechanical hoist bucket filled from small coal tubs manoeuvred along an adjacent narrow gauge rail line. The tubs had previously been filled from locomotive coal wagons stabled in a siding along the rear of the coaling facility.

The coaling arrangements epitomised the generally poorly equipped facilities and track layout at the depot, which seem to have evolved rather than been designed to facilitate the logical through movement of locomotives as servicing progressed. This was not helped by the depot being located within the confines of the triangle, limiting further expansion. Former footplate staff recalled double shunts being necessary for many engine movements between the coaling stage, Passenger and Goods sheds. Congestion and delays to engines going off shed could occur at busy times. Given that this was the Motive Power District's principal 'A' shed, with a large ninety-two engines allocation in 1948, still boasting seventy-seven engines in 1960, one would have expected to have seen the sort of investment that had been made by the GWR at other main depots during the Churchward era and Government Loans period. By 1960, with dieselisation looming, the horse had long since bolted. The Churchward era had seen new roundhouse depots built at Old Oak Common, Tyseley, Oxley, Newport Ebbw Junction and Bristol St Phillip's Marsh and a little later Stourbridge Junction. There had

also been some major investment in enlarged standard coaling stages along with depot track remodelling at a number of depots in the 1920/30s. The Worcester District's Gloucester Horton Road had seen major investment during that period and one is left wondering why Worcester missed out. In fact, a number of draft schemes were drawn up over the years, for which there is not room here to go into detail. None ever got past the drawing board stage, some inexplicably and others through bad timing due to the intervention of world wars or rail nationalisation.

Continuing with the depot's general operational arrangements, the Passenger Shed's primary role was the immediate servicing of locomotives after coaling was completed. This was where visiting engines on short turnarounds would usually be found awaiting their next duty. The Passenger Shed was particularly convenient for engines taking up passenger working from Shrub Hill and notably those for Paddington services. Some servicing and preparation also occurred at the front of the Goods Shed, particularly for local shunting and trip engines and those stood down for longer periods overnight.

The Goods Shed was where mileage and periodic scheduled maintenance and boiler washouts took place. A stationary boiler was located outside the building, providing hot water for boiler washouts connected to pipes and hoses distributed at key points through the building. All four shed roads had locomotive pits and these projected outside the rear of the shed. There light and even moderately heavy repairs were undertaken. It was not unusual to find failed visiting engines there awaiting attention. Much of this repair work was undertaken in the open, exposed to prevailing weather conditions, although it was said staff preferred this location to working in the damp and oppressive confines of the shed. Should lifting or heavier repairs be required, engines were sent over to the Locomotive Works on the far side of the main line. The shed stores supplied smaller and consumable parts whilst larger items were requested from the Locomotive Works stores.

Along the inside wall of the Goods Shed was the said depot stores as well as a large mess room for drivers and firemen. This was the gathering point for meal breaks for both home based and visiting footplate crews, where they would await orders on forward services from the Shift Running Foreman. Strict hierarchy applied amongst the staff and the depot's young locomotive cleaners, for which there was still an establishment of twenty in 1961, were not permitted in the drivers and firemen's mess room. This was despite many being passed for and regularly upgraded to firing duties. These youngsters were at the bottom of the depot pecking order and relegated to their own rather dilapidated carriage body mess room outside the back of the Goods Shed. A new mess room was later built in that area for all footplate staff. Cleaners were never the less an important part of the depot staffing. This youthful group, under the watchful eye of fatherly Charge Hand Cleaner Fred Jones, were, amongst other duties, responsible for cleaning the depot's fleet of 'Castle' class locomotives for Paddington express passenger duties.

There was no road access to the depot, located as it was within Worcester's railway triangle. The main pedestrian access was via an elevated footbridge over the line from Railway Walk and through a door in the footpath fence. This led directly to the depot's administration offices. These were located on either side of a long internal passageway leading to steps down to the Goods Shed. Hung along the passage walls were glass cases containing enginemen's rosters, daily alterations, speed and other notices. Doors led from the passageway into the Chief Clerk's and Shed Master's personal offices and another where roster and stores clerks were located. On the other side of the passage was a large office where staff booked on and off duty through a hatch and where the all-important Shed Running Foreman, Timekeeper and several other clerks were based. Cleaners on callboy duty and a messenger also shared this office.

Worcester, being the District's 'A' shed, was where breakdown vans and a heavy duty breakdown crane were located for derailments and other specialised lifting duties. Until 1961, the depot crane was Cowan & Sheldon No 9, a thirty-five tons steam crane built in 1913 and originally owned by the Rhymney Railway in South Wales. This was replaced in 1961 by another Cowan & Sheldon thirty-five tons steam crane re-located from Banbury. This had an equally long history having been built for the Taff Vale Railway in 1911. I'm sure few at the time realised the historic significance of these silently stabled practical giants. Not to be forgotten, small rail mounted steam crane No 43 was used in the yard for loading spent locomotive ash to steel lined wagons for disposal. Once again, this task demonstrated the absence of mechanical aids at the depot, in this case for clearing this essential daily waste. To be fair, this was a general deficiency at most ex-GWR depots, unlike the more modern facilities to be found in particular at ex-LMS sheds, including not far away at Bristol Barrow Road, which had a mechanical ash clearing plant.

Worcester Passenger Shed at the departure end for Shrub Hill station on 20 September 1964 with an LMR engine's tender protruding from the shed building. A youthful number taker emerges from between recently withdrawn Worcester 'Castle' No 7025 *Sudeley Castle* (withdrawn 5.9.64) and another 'Castle' and 4MT 2-6-2 prairie tank. MANCHESTER LOCOMOTIVE SOCIETY

Worcester Passenger Shed, with the depot's rather careworn No 7013 *Bristol Castle* ready to come off to work a Paddington service. Another 4-6-0 is stood on the adjacent road, whilst the left hand side clearly illustrates the through nature of the shed building. NORMAN HARROP COLLECTION. MANCHESTER LOCOMOTIVE SOCIETY

Worcester Passenger Shed viewed from the opposite end with Worcester's No 7025 *Sudeley Castle,* having just finished coaling, running forward to go through the shed ready to work the next Paddington service. The Goods Shed can be seen on the right, along with its prominent stationary boiler and chimney whilst an unidentified visiting Hughes 6P/5F 'Crab' 2-6-0 and local 0-6-0 pannier tanks 3F No 4628 and 2F No 1639 stable in the centre. The photograph is taken from high up on the coaling hoist. R.C. Riley. Transport Treasury

The Coaling Hoist was a non-standard electrically operated Stothert and Pitt design installed in 1944. The coaling of Worcester's No 7005 *Sir Edward Elgar* is overseen by a staff member on 17 February 1962, the engine boasting whitewashed buffers suggesting a recent special train working. John Goss

The Coaling Hoist in close-up with Pontypool Road's 5MT 4-6-0 No 6872 *Crawley Grange* being replenished in April 1964. The engine would have previously worked a freight service from Pontypool Road via Hereford. TIM FAREBROTHER

Goods Engine Shed on the far right of the site with its stationary boiler and chimney prominent. The date is 6 June 1963 and local Worcester based engines on view are 2F 0-6-0PT No 1639, 4MT 2-6-2T No 4113 and 5MT 4-6-0 No 6992 *Arborfield Hall*. R.C. Riley. Transport Treasury

Rear of the Goods Shed where locomotive repairs exposed to the elements were undertaken. Far from home, Croes Newydd's 8F 2-8-0 No 3817 has clearly failed whilst on freight working through the area and awaits repair on 15 November 1964. Ralph Ward

Framed inside the Shed are Worcester engines 3MT 0-6-0 No 2246 and 7P 4-6-0 No 7031 *Cromwell's Castle* in February 1963. Both are ready for their next turn of duty. RAILPHOTOPRINTS

From Railway Walk looking down at engines stabled at the front of the Goods Shed on 9 May 1963. This was a prime viewing point, nostalgically remembered by a generation of young Worcester enthusiasts. Featured are local 2F 0-6-0PTs Nos 1639 and 1661, the latter with spark arrester chimney, a 4MT 2-6-2 prairie tank and Oxley's 5MT 4-6-0 No 6828 *Trellech Grange* off an inwards freight working. Meanwhile, a withdrawn ex-GWR railcar lies in the background. Easily recognisable fitter Frank Waters, with his ever present shoulder-slung long-handled hammer, exchanges pleasantries with another staff member. BEN ASHWORTH

Former Shed Turntable, long disused, in the only surviving image found of this long forgotten feature. Taken in the 1940s, it is already disused although its main elements are still visible. The siding on which it is located runs parallel with the side of the triangle from Rainbow Hill Junction to Tunnel Junction. K.G. MARLING. CHRISTOPHER WILKINSON COLLECTION

Steam Crane No 43 on 17 December 1963 in Worcester's shed yard loading spent locomotive ash to a metal sided wagon for disposal. Even using the crane this was a slow labour intensive operation crying out for more sophisticated mechanisation. D. CLAYTON. ANDREW SMITH COLLECTION

Worcester Footplate and Shed Staff

Driver Peter Jackson. How better to start this section than with this 1964 photograph of Worcester driver Peter Jackson. The image says it all in terms of dedication, length of service and job experience. A top link driver, he is pictured at Worcester on the footplate of the depot's favourite 'Castle' 4-6-0 No 7005 *Sir Edward Elgar*. ROY SMITH. TED RUDD COLLECTION

We tend to regard the locomotives themselves as the living, breathing heart of a steam depot and indeed their detail is generally well preserved. However all too often the parallel story of the shed and footplate staff that kept these engines running is allowed to slip away unrecorded. This is often because few recorded memories remain, but in Worcester's case there is still a long held tradition of former shed and footplate staff meeting and reminiscing as an organised group. I feel privileged to have been able to tap into those memories and record for others how the depot functioned in practice and some of the characters that made up what was known as the railway community. They worked in difficult times in the 1960s, with variable job security and indifferent working conditions as steam motive power's reign drew to a close. With it went a long history of tradition and practice.

The Shed Master, who reported direct to the District Running and Maintenance Officer, was in overall charge of the depot. In 1960, the district's two senior shed masters were Harry Cureton at Worcester overseeing a fleet of seventy-seven steam locomotives and Sam Knowles, thirty miles down the line at Gloucester Horton Road, with a fleet of eighty-four engines; both places major ex-GWR locomotive depots. A grade lower was Fred Cole at the ex-Midland Railway's Gloucester Barnwood. He had a much smaller fleet of thirty-two engines, but oversaw a comparatively large footplate staff relieving through passenger and freight services between Bristol, Birmingham New Street and Derby. Fred Cole would later become a central figure in the Worcester shed story. All three had extensive Running and Maintenance experience, although Fred Cole was by some years the youngest of the three.

Worcester would experience remarkable consistency in its shed master's service, with just two occupying the role between 1950 and January 1966 steam depot closure. Harry Cureton, who had been appointed in 1950, was from the West Midlands and a former Tyseley driver who had risen through the supervisory ranks to this management role. He was remembered by his office staff for regularly ordering a favourite dripping cake to accompany his morning cup of tea. It would be fetched by the office boy on his bike from the local baker. Harry Cureton was regarded as old school and a solid and safe if at times sticky pair of hands. He would retire after a lifetime's railway career in 1964.

Harry Cureton would be succeeded by Fred Cole on promotion from Gloucester Barnwood. This rather conveniently coincided with Gloucester Barnwood's May 1964 depot closure; its locomotives and footplate staff merged into the adjacent Gloucester Horton Road shed that was still under Sam Knowles' control.

Fred Cole was well respected by both management and staff and was known for his tactful but firm handling of workplace issues. He had the difficult task of managing Worcester's steam depot closure, but would provide continuity by becoming the first Area Traincrew Manager, now responsible for both drivers and guards, in the new world of multi-functional Area Management. He would just prior to retirement be given the prized role of Area Manager Worcester. The Western Region's General Manager Leslie Lloyd wrote to him in 1979, just after Fred's retirement:

'When I arrived at Worcester the other day I naturally asked if "Mr. Worcester" was about, for you have always represented what is good about that part of the world. I was staggered to learn that you had gone on retirement two weeks ago.'

Shed Master Harry Cureton poses proudly on the footplate of No 6937 *Conyngham Hall* on shed at Worcester on 26 March 1964. This was probably taken to mark his retirement. A former Tyseley driver, he had risen through the supervisory ranks and was Worcester's shed master from 1950 to 1964 retirement. ROY SMITH. TERRY GURD COLLECTION

Leslie Lloyd went on to thank him for all he had done over the years and invited him up to Paddington for a one to one farewell meal.

It is easy to forget the large staffing and the broad skills base that was involved in running a motive power depot. In 1961, shed master Harry Cureton was responsible for no less than 428 staff. This included a footplate establishment at Worcester itself of 164 drivers (all posts filled), 133 firemen (of which twenty-eight were vacancies) and twenty cleaners (of which six were vacancies). There were a further twenty-six footplate staff out-based at Evesham, Kingham, Honeybourne and Ledbury sub-sheds. The depot's servicing and maintenance staff were split into two groups; non-trade registered locomotive servicing personnel and the trade skilled mechanical staff. In 1960 the locomotive servicing staff establishment numbered forty-six (of which twelve or 26 per cent were vacancies). These comprised a chargeman engine cleaner, boiler washers, fire droppers, steam raisers, coalmen, stores issuers, tube cleaners and tool men. The only out-based servicing staff were two fire droppers at Honeybourne and one coal man at Kingham. The skilled mechanical staff establishment numbered fifty-three (of which nine – or 16 per cent – were vacancies). They comprised a chargeman fitter, fitters, fitters' assistants, chargeman boiler smith, boiler smiths, boiler smiths' assistants, ATC electricians, general electricians, apprentice fitters and apprentice boiler smiths. Also listed within this group were a shop officeman and a mess room attendant.

General Manager,
Western Region,
British Railways,
Paddington Station,
London W2 1HA.

L. Lloyd

Tel. 01-723 7000 Ext. 2819

10th August, 1979

F. Cole, Esq.,
362 Ombersley Road,
WORCESTER,
WR3 7HE

Dear Mr Cole,

     When I arrived at Worcester the
other day I naturally asked if "Mr. Worcester"
was about because, to me, you have always
represented all that is good about that part
of the world. I was staggered to learn that
you had gone on retirement two weeks ago.

     The purpose of this letter is,
therefore, two-fold. Firstly to say thank
you for all that you have done for the Region
over many years and, secondly, to ask if you
would be good enough to come up and have lunch
with me here some time in the near future.

Yours sincerely,

Leslie Lloyd

Shed Master Fred Cole had just retired as Area Manager Worcester in 1979 when he received this glowing testimony from Western Region General Manager Leslie Lloyd. Fred is sadly no longer with us, but he safely kept this letter throughout his retirement. FRED COLE COLLECTION

Shed Office Staff in October 1964. Standing left to right are John Summers, Hugh Lamour, Bill Shepherd, Harry Collins, Ben Lewis, Steve James and Peter Westwood. Seated are Chief Clerk Alan Barber, Shed Master Fred Cole and Joe Bridgwater. FRED COLE COLLECTION

Skittles Team Winners in the 1960s. Sporting competitions between stations and depots, mostly organised through the British Rail Staff Association, were a regular part of the railway social calendar. Here my father George Bartlett, the District Running and Maintenance Officer, second from right, has just presented a skittles trophy to the Worcester depot team. WORCESTER RAILWAY SOCIETY

The Shed Master's office staff comprised a chief clerk, four shift running foremen working around the clock, a roster clerk, stores clerk, engine history clerk, timekeepers and a small administration support. The shift running foremen were responsible for the allocation of locomotives to train services in conjunction with District Control and ensuring that engines and their footplate crews left the depot on time and to plan. Like the swan that glided gracefully on the surface, but was paddling furiously under the water, they achieved this in the face of increasingly unpredictable times. Steam locomotive condition was becoming increasingly challenging, there would be regular short term footplate crew alterations to cope with late running freight services or the cancellation of inwards workings leading to the juggling of staff and locomotive resources. Footplate staff also required a minimum of twelve hours rest before their next turn of duty. At times of disruption, this could lead to crews having to be stepped up to cover those booking on duty late after minimum rest. Shed running foremen needed to know their staff well, including those that would only work bare hours and those who were prepared to take on extra work late in their shift with overtime in prospect. Former young firemen recall how it could be frustrating when they would have welcomed overtime, but were working with a driver who was reluctant to exceed his booked hours. Well remembered running shed foremen included Percy Cunnington, Noel Higgins, Ivor Cotterell, Fred Bennett and Harry Powell; the latter affectionately known by the youngsters as Uncle Harry. On the panel, as it was known at ex-GWR depots, were volunteer senior drivers who were trained and willing to act as relief shed foremen when required. These included Sid Neil, Ken Alford, Reggie Dancocks and Jack (or some say John) Saunders.

Returning to the previously described depot staffing numbers, a surprising element, given the perception this was a contracting railway system with much redundancy, was the number of staff vacancies at the time. Indeed in 1960, whilst Worcester's driver establishment was full, there were no less than thirty-four firemen and engine cleaners' vacancies and twenty-one shed servicing and mechanical staff vacancies. The situation with firemen and engine cleaners was of particular concern, with no less than a twenty-five per cent vacancy gap. This undoubtedly put a strain on the depot's day to day working with reliance on upgrading, overtime and staff goodwill. Redundancy for many would come in later years but the reality in 1960 was that, even in a provincial city like Worcester, there was significant outside job vacancy competition. Many of these industries offered warmer, cleaner, better paid working conditions with regular working hours. Railway work was at the time perceived as poorly paid in comparison with elsewhere. A government report into railway pay in 1960 led to noticeable improvements in pay rates during the next few years. However, despite these shortcomings, there remained a dedicated and mostly time served staff, supported by a surprisingly large number of younger, often teenage, recruits. Junior firemen were indeed being promoted very quickly from the starting grade of engine cleaner, into which in turn early school leavers were still being recruited.

The depot's flagship services, the Hereford-Worcester-Paddington expresses, were worked by the most senior and experienced top link drivers and likewise time served firemen. These workings would become the last regularly steam hauled express passenger service into Paddington and until the final few years, Worcester still turned out sparkling clean engines with polished brass work. This was achieved under the watchful eye of foreman engine cleaner Fred Jones long after other depots had abandoned routine engine cleaning.

The diagrammed workload for Worcester's 164 drivers and 133 firemen would have been broken down into meaningful chunks or links of work within an overall link structure. Each link contained a designated number of men who would rotate their duties over a period of weeks. This was typically twelve lines of six days work with a further two lines of rest day relief coverage, making altogether fourteen weeks work around which footplate staff rotated. The links were organised sequentially in seniority order, with individuals moving up the links as vacancies occurred. The top links covered express passenger work, with in descending order long distance freight work, of which due to work quantity there were several links, and then a combination of local passenger, branch line passenger, freight tripping and finally yard and station shunting duties. There was also a restricted shed link for accommodating drivers with health or main line restricted issues. The senior links might also contain some mixed work to ensure a more balanced shift pattern, make efficient use of spare time at the end of a shift or to optimise route knowledge.

Route knowledge was expensive to acquire and maintain and the link structure would be designed to ensure drivers passed over each route within the minimum required frequency to ensure route knowledge was maintained. Some experienced drivers might carry wider or more specialised route knowledge than was directly required in their link. This could be advantageous to the shift running foreman at times of service disruption or where special train working was required. Often, such drivers took great pride in their wider route knowledge and would proactively ensure this was maintained by requesting refresher turns when necessary.

It goes without saying that such versatility could at times bring high earning potential generating significant overtime.

The depot's locomotives' range of operation was very obvious to the rail enthusiast, who soon noticed when different depot's engines started to appear on a specific service. However, there were no similar clues as to how far footplate crews were working, particularly when taking over other depots' engines on through trains and in particular on long distance freight services. Through talking to former Worcester footplate staff I have managed to put together a reasonably comprehensive route knowledge for the depot with some freight service knowledge revealing a few surprises.

Passenger route knowledge was held over all the main routes radiating from Worcester and it was just a question of how far Worcester crews travelled. In summary, this was Worcester to Paddington, Hereford, Birmingham Snow Hill (via both Kidderminster and Stratford-upon-Avon), Leamington Spa, Birmingham New Street (via Bromsgrove) and Gloucester Eastgate. All were ex-GWR routes, except for the former Midland Railway workings to Gloucester Eastgate and Birmingham New Street. This passenger work had been absorbed into the main depot in 1958 when a small link of Gloucester Barnwood out-based crews, their separate existence going back to Midland Railway days, were absorbed into the main Worcester depot. The several branch lines were also covered.

It may come as a surprise to those less familiar with Worcester that the depot's drivers also worked passenger services on the Severn Valley routes between Kidderminster-Bridgnorth-Shrewsbury, Hartlebury-Bewdley and also Bewdley-Tenbury Wells-Woofferton. Despite there being some loco-hauled passenger services worked by Kidderminster and Shrewsbury crews, the majority of the services over the Severn Valley lines were worked by ex-GWR diesel railcars. These came out empty stock from Worcester each morning and returning to the depot each night, with Worcester drivers staying with them throughout the day on all the Severn Valley lines. In the early 1950s, Worcester drivers even signed the Hereford to Shrewsbury main line in order to work an early morning empty stock from Worcester to Woofferton via Ledbury and Shelwick Junction (reverse) in order to start up the morning service from there. In the early 1950s, they also worked back a passenger service at the end of the day from Shrewsbury over the now long-closed Leominster to Bromyard branch section and from there into Worcester. These two rather extreme workings had disappeared by 1960.

Whilst Worcester engines had a reasonable amount of long distance freight work, the depot's footplate crews ranged far and wide on through trains worked by other depots' engines. This gave Worcester a varied and extensive freight route knowledge that significantly exceeded passenger work. This included Worcester to Wolverhampton Low Level and Oxley Yard (via Stourbridge and the Dudley to Wolverhampton branch line). Some crews even worked beyond Oxley to Crewe (via Market Drayton). Indeed, photographs exist of Worcester engines on shed at the small ex-GWR Crewe Gresty Road depot. Other freight work took Worcester crews to Oxford's Yarnton and Hinksey yards, to Hereford on South Wales bound services and to Stourbridge Junction and West Midlands' yards beyond. Looking westwards, freight services were worked to Gloucester both via Honeybourne and Cheltenham Malvern Road and via Abbotts Wood Junction and Ashchurch. Many crews worked beyond there to the ex-GWR Stoke Gifford yard via Yate. Former footplate men recall they also signed the route into Bristol to take engines from Stoke Gifford for servicing

at St Phillip's Marsh shed. Finally there were several starting freight trains from Worcester taking the ex-Midland Railway route from Droitwich via Bromsgrove and the Lickey Incline to Birmingham's Washwood Heath yard and Lawley Street.

There was a laid down career structure for younger footplate staff to build up experience and knowledge in readiness for promotion to driver. Senior firemen would be trained as 'passed drivers' for flexibly upgrading to driver duties as required. Similarly the depot's cleaners would, providing they were old enough to work shifts, be trained as 'passed firemen'. They could be similarly upgraded although this was usually to the least demanding work such as yard or station pilot duties. However, at times of real shortage, or particularly it seemed on Saturdays, they could find themselves thrown in at the deep end covering a main line local passenger turn. Drivers' personalities varied considerably and still over fifty years later there are clear memories of how as nervous new boys they might be met on the footplate. Most drivers would welcome the newcomer and gently ease them in to the job and sometimes even help them with the firing. However, a few drivers could be lacking in patience when landed with a 'rookie' and might meet the newcomer with a frosty stare and little practical advice. Driving styles varied considerably and several former cleaners/firemen had similar stories to tell regarding one Worcester driver, Charlie Huntley. I'm sure he was a delightful man at home, but at work he was known as having only one way of driving and that was hard and aggressive whether the schedule required it or not. Several recalled coming back at the end of a shift with him dirty, dishevelled and exhausted. This was despite footplate inspectors emphasising the importance of an economic firing and driving technique.

A TRIBUTE TO WORCESTER SHED STAFF

Worcester Shed Cleaners in about 1964. Chargeman cleaner Fred Jones is pictured with four of his young charges: Chris Smith, Alan Collins, Brian Parsons and Rob Hemming. How young they all seem and would no doubt have been a youthful handful for Fred Jones to oversee. Who do you think looks most mischievous? FRED COLE COLLECTION

Fitter Frank Waters, a well-remembered depot character, is pictured on 8 January 1964 in the locomotive pit complete with cap at jaunty angle, pipe as ever in his mouth and his trade mark long handled hammer. A depot boiler washer poses alongside. No 7011 *Banbury Castle* had been transferred from Reading to Worcester that week. R.G. NELSON/TERRY WALSH

Worcester Shed Staff in front of the depot's No 7011 *Banbury Castle*. The photo is undated but the engine was Worcester-based from October 1960 to October 1962 and January to June 1964. Posing left to right are Jeff Yates, Peter Kitson, George Robbins, Jack Saunders, Ron 'Bomber' Harris and Ken Alford. MANCHESTER LOCOMOTIVE SOCIETY. BILL GWYTHEN COLLECTION

Farewell to Steam. No 7023 *Penrice Castle* smartly turned out on 7 September 1963 to work the last scheduled steam working to London; the 10.05am Hereford to Paddington forward from Worcester. In the event, the winter 1963/64 timetable largely reverted back to steam haulage due to a serious diesel shortfall. Worcester shed staff featured include fourth from left fireman Mick Rock, far right chargeman cleaner Fred Jones and second from right acting shed running foreman Reg Dancox. MICK ROCK

Driver Sid Haynes and his youthful looking fireman Brian Houseman with Worcester's No 7023 *Penrice Castle* ready to depart with the previously mentioned 10.05am. Hereford to Paddington from Worcester on 7 September 1963. WORCESTER LOCOMOTIVE SOCIETY

Footplate Inspector Harold Cook, an experienced headquarters locomotive inspector dressed in overalls and beret, with Worcester driver Peter Jackson and fireman Roy Cale. Their Paddington to Hereford service, headed by Worcester's No 7025 *Sudeley Castle*, has paused at Oxford on 31 May 1963. Well respected photographer Dick Riley has persuaded the crew to pose for him during the short break. R.C. RILEY. TRANSPORT TREASURY

No 7027 *Thornbury Castle* in pristine condition at Worcester Works having been prepared to work a Colwall to Paddington Royal Train on 23 June 1960 taking HRH Queen Elizabeth the Queen Mother back from the Three Counties Show at Malvern. Worcester Works and Shed staff gathered for this official photo and a framed copy stood on my father's desk in his District Running and Maintenance Officer's office and now sits on my desk as these notes are written. WORCESTER LOCOMOTIVE SOCIETY COLLECTION.

DMU Driver Training. 'Where do you put the coal then?' might have been the jocular exchange as Worcester driver Jim Teal chats to tutor driver Bill Shuard, driver Len Long and passenger guard Arthur Savage. They are ready to join the DMU on Shrub Hill station's centre road for driver training. STEVE BARTLETT COLLECTION

Driver Allen Tapper with fireman Doug Hatton on the footplate of another Worcester 'Castle' favourite No 7007 *Great Western* on 3 November 1962. He was another old hand top link driver and a regular on the Paddington services. ROY SMITH. TERRY RUDD COLLECTION

Driver Geoff Truby on the footplate with fireman Tim O'Grady perched on the tender of Didcot's 5MT 4-6-0 No 6937 *Conyngham Hall* ready to work a Paddington service forward from Worcester on 27 March 1964. ROY SMITH. TERRY RUDD COLLECTION

Dougie Davies with a colleague servicing Worcester's No 7031 *Cromwell's Castle*. The photo is undated but the engine was based at Worcester from February 1962 to July 1963. ROY SMITH. TERRY RUDD COLLECTION

Worcester's Locomotive Allocation

As locomotive whistles sounded to welcome in the 1 January 1960 New Year it was to a still steam engine dominated Worcester area. Collett 7P 'Castle' 4-6-0s dominated Hereford-Worcester-Paddington services, whilst steam locomotives also handled all freight trains passing through the area. Shunting duties in the yards, local freight trips and the majority of secondary passenger services were also still in the hands of steam traction. Ironically, local passenger services had been partially diesel operated since the 1930s using Great Western Railway diesel railcars. There were still seven of these based at Worcester in 1960; the largest single depot allocation remaining. New generation diesel multiple units did however now operate many of the semi-fast Cardiff-Hereford-Worcester Foregate Street-Birmingham Snow Hill services. This was the only route where dieselisation had impacted to any degree. These trains had previously been mostly worked by Cardiff Canton, Tyseley and Hereford based 5MT 'Hall' 4-6-0s

and their loss had little impact on Worcester's allocation. Later in 1960, however, the first diesel shunting engines would appear; comparatively late arrivals compared with the large numbers that had been arriving in other areas since the mid-1950s.

We start our look at Worcester's locomotive allocation in January 1960, then numbering seventy-seven steam engines. These comprised ten 7P 'Castle' 4-6-0s, nine 5MT 'Hall' 4-6-0s, five 5MT 'Modified Hall' 4-6-0s, five 5MT 'Grange' 4-6-0s, two 4MT BR Standard 75000 4-6-0s, one 4MT 4300 2-6-0, ten 3MT 2251 0-6-0 tender engines (of which two were in store), three 2MT BR Standard 78000 2-6-0s, seven 4MT 5101 2-6-2Ts, one 4MT 8100 2-6-2T, one 3MT BR Standard 82000 2-6-2T, eleven 4F 9400 0-6-0PTs, ten 3F 5700 0-6-0PTs and two 2F 1600 0-6-0PTs. The detailed allocation is set out in the adjacent table.

Looking first at material changes that had occurred over the previous four years since January 1956, the overall allocation had reduced from eighty-eight to seventy-seven locomotives. Whilst there had been little evidence of dieselisation or line closures affecting the depot during the period, there must have been some reductions in freight and local passenger services. The principal losses were confined to just three areas. There had been a reduction from ten to just a single Churchward 4MT 4300 2-6-0, the last three Churchward 4MT 4500 2-6-2Ts had gone and also the last four 1P 1400 and 5800 0-4-2Ts. The 1400s had previously shared in auto-train mode Bromyard branch and some main line local passenger services with ex-GWR diesel railcars and 4MT prairie tanks. The latter two types now covered the services previously worked by these smaller 0-4-2Ts.

85A Worcester
Allocation 2 January 1960

'Castle' 7P 4-6-0	75000 4MT 4-6-0	82000 3MT 2-6-2T
4088 *Dartmouth Castle*	75003	82008
4089 *Donnington Castle*	75025	Total: 1
5037 *Monmouth Castle*	Total: 2	
5039 *Rhuddlan Castle*		9400 4F 0-6-0PT
5042 *Winchester Castle*	4300 4MT 2-6-0	8427
5071 *Spitfire*	5396	8460
5081 *Lockheed Hudson*	Total: 1	8480
7002 *Devizes Castle*		8496
7005 *Sir Edward Elgar*	2251 3MT 0-6-0	9401
7007 *Great Western*	2209	9429
Total:10	2243	9455
	2247	9466
'Hall' 5MT 4-6-0	2273	9475
4907 *Broughton Hall*	3205	9480
4993 *Dalton Hall*	3213	9486
4996 *Eden Hall*	3214	Total: 11
5917 *Westminster Hall*	3216 (stored)	
5994 *Roydon Hall*	3217 (stored)	5700 3F 0-6-0PT
5996 *Mytton Hall*	3218	3605
6947 *Helmingham Hall*	Total: 10	3607
6948 *Holbrooke Hall*		3725
6950 *Kingsthorpe Hall*	78000 2MT 2-6-0	3775
Total: 9	78001	4613
	78008	4614
'Modified Hall' 5MT 4-6-0	78009	4625
6984 *Owsden Hall*	Total: 3	4664
6989 *Wightwick Hall*		7707
6992 *Arborfield Hall*	5101 4MT 2-6-2T	7777
7920 *Coney Hall*	4109	Total: 10
7928 *Wolf Hall*	4113	
Total: 5	4124	1600 2F 0-6-0PT
	4142	1629
'Grange' 5MT 4-6-0	4152	1661
6807 *Birchwood Grange*	5110	Total: 2
6820 *Kingstone Grange*	5179	
6851 *Hurst Grange*	Total: 7	**Total Steam:** 77
6856 *Stowe Grange*		(inc. 2 stored)
6877 *Llanfair Grange*	8100 4MT 2-6-2T	
Total:5	8106	
	Total: 1	

On the heavy freight locomotive side the last four Churchward 8F 2800s and a single 5MT Collett 'Manor' 4-6-0 had gone, replaced by an equivalent number of 5MT 'Hall' and 'Grange' 4-6-0s, plus two recently built 4MT BR Standard 75000 4-6-0s. On the positive side the depot's flagship 7P 'Castle' 4-6-0s had increased from seven to ten locomotives and a similar proportionate increase had occurred at the District's other large depot, Gloucester Horton Road. These changes were not driven by an increase in express passenger work but linked to the first diesel hydraulic arrivals deposing 'Castles' from the principal Paddington to West of England and Bristol services. This enabled more to be cascaded to depots where they might not previously have been spared.

We will next move on to material changes over the following two years from January 1960 to February 1962. In the intervening period little had changed around Worcester to the casual railway observer. Paddington services were still all steam hauled and almost all long distance freight services similarly so, as was all local freight trip working. Worcester, however, had since late 1960 acquired a small allocation of five 204hp diesel mechanical (later class 03) shunting engines. These were covering four shunting turns, whilst the fifth engine was held spare. Their duties embraced Worcester's three freight yard pilots, whilst a fourth was out-based at Evesham. Partly due to this, the small steam sub-shed there had closed in June 1961, although four drivers were still retained there. The only noticeable change on the passenger side was an increasing presence of diesel multiple units, including the single car variants. These were steadily replacing steam-hauled local services and the depot's ex-GWR railcars. The latter would be finally eliminated from Worcester in October 1962; the last depot to operate these iconic and popular vehicles. The GWR publicity machine had made much of their initial introduction in the 1930s. The early vehicles acquired the nickname of 'flying bananas' due to their streamlined shape and chocolate and cream livery. The ex-GWR railcars operations in the Worcester area deserve a closer look and they are given their own chapter later in the book.

By 24 February 1962, Worcester's allocation was down to sixty-one engines comprising nine 7P 'Castle' 4-6-0s, eight 5MT 'Hall' 4-6-0s, five 5MT 'Modified Hall' 4-6-0s, five 5MT 'Grange' 4-6-0s, two 4MT BR Standard 75000 4-6-0s, six 4MT 4300 2-6-0s, three 8F 5205 2-8-0Ts, two 5MT 5600 0-6-2Ts (both in store), three 3MT 2251 0-6-0 tender engines, two 2MT BR Standard 78000 2-6-0s, two 4MT 5101 2-6-2Ts, two 4MT 8100 2-6-2Ts, five 4F 9400 0-6-0PTs, five 3F 5700 0-6-0PTs and two 2F 1600 0-6-0PTs. The detailed allocation is set out in a separate table at the end of the chapter. This was a reduction of fifteen locomotives since January 1960. Principal changes included five fewer 3F 5700 pannier tanks, following the introduction of diesel shunting engines, and six fewer 4F 9400 pannier tanks. The latter cull was from an excessive January 1960 allocation of eleven engines. The over provision of this rather unnecessary and comparatively late tank engine build had seen a number declared surplus to requirements and put into store at Worcester and up the road at Kidderminster, where there was surplus storage siding accommodation. Worcester's Nos 8460, 8496, 9455 and 9466 were noted in store with bagged chimneys at Kidderminster in September 1960 but would soon all be withdrawn or moved on elsewhere. There had also been a net reduction of four 4MT 2-6-2Ts through a combination of increased DMU coverage on main line local passenger services and changes in freight tripping arrangements. It is noticeable that over the years the choice of locomotive classes for freight trip working in the area changed on a number of occasions. Along with the aforementioned reduction in 4F 9400 0-6-0PTs and 4MT 5101 2-6-2Ts there were also in February 1962 seven less 3MT 2251 0-6-0s. These losses were however balanced by five extra 4MT 4300 2-6-0s and three 8F 5205 2-8-0Ts. The latter had arrived in 1960, when parent shed responsibility for banking duties at the Ledbury sub-shed was transferred from Hereford to Worcester. One of these heavy tank engines would spend all week on banking duties, whilst a second was diagrammed for freight work from main depot Worcester. The third engine provided spare cover for this small specialist allocation.

Moving on a further eighteen months to October 1963, this was now a railway with diesel traction much more in evidence. The Worcester allocation was significantly now down to thirty-nine engines compared with sixty-two in February 1962. This comprised five 7P 'Castle' 4-6-0s (one of which was in store), one 5MT 'Hall' 4-6-0, four 5MT 'Modified Hall' 4-6-0s, five 5MT 'Grange' 4-6-0s, two 4MT BR Standard 75000 4-6-0s, three 8F 5205 2-8-0Ts, three 3MT 2251 0-6-0 tender engines, one 2MT BR Standard 78000 2-6-0, two 4MT 5101 2-6-2Ts, one 4MT 6100 2-6-2T, two 4MT 8100 2-6-2Ts, two 4F 9400 0-6-0PTs, six 3F 5700 0-6-0PTs and two 2F 1600 0-6-0PTs. The detailed allocation is once again set out in a table at the end of the chapter. The shed had lost a third of its allocation in the last eighteen months but, despite this, the remaining engines still played an important part in the local railway scene. Indeed, the shed still seemed busy, including hosting a varied selection of visiting freight engines. However, the very visible line of withdrawn engines on shed sidings awaiting disposal couldn't be avoided. In some respects, this did not reflect the true degree of lost work. A number of them had been withdrawn, not due to loss of work but high mileage, with works attention denied or alternatively

mechanical failure exceeding repair expenditure limits. They had in these cases been replaced by transfers in from other depots although these were not always in much better condition.

The heaviest losses between February 1962 and October 1963 were amongst the large tender engines. Driver traction training on main line diesels had started on D7000 'Hymek', Type 3 diesel hydraulics early on in 1963. This was usually undertaken on service workings, initially between Worcester and Hereford. 'Hymeks' were soon regularly working through to Paddington on scheduled work, although extra drivers were often on board undergoing traction training in parallel. By October 1963, the 'Castle' allocation had fallen from nine to five, with one of these actually in store. Similarly the 'Hall' and 'Modified Hall' allocation had fallen from thirteen to just five engines, although there was still an unchanged five 'Granges' at the depot. All six of the depot's 4MT 4300 2-6-0s had departed; a class that had built back up in recent years after its earlier cull. These reductions either moved on to pastures new or to that great scrapyard in the sky. Tank engine classes however only saw minor changes during the period.

Main line freight trains passing through the area were in October 1963 still mainly steam hauled and local freight trips almost exclusively so. However, DMUs now worked almost all local passenger services, with the exception of one Bromyard branch trip and one Worcester prairie tank turn on a late afternoon local service to Malvern and Ledbury. A Kidderminster or Stourbridge Junction prairie tank also passed through Foregate Street in the late afternoon on a local passenger service to Ledbury. The summer 1963 timetable had seen mixed traction on Paddington services, with complete 'Hymek' operation scheduled for September 1963, coincidental with the commencement of the winter timetable. A final Worcester 'Castle' run was officially organised on the last Saturday and photographed by the local newspaper. However within weeks diesel availability elsewhere on the Western Region amongst Type 4 'Warship' and 'Western' diesel hydraulics went from bad to worse and the route's 'Hymeks' were increasingly taken away to cover shortfalls elsewhere. How the depot coped during this difficult period with an already reduced 'Castle' allocation, plus some additional engines on loan, is covered in a later chapter.

A surprising earlier sight at Worcester in February 1963 had been a Southern Region Birmingham RC&W Type 3 D6500 class diesel. This had caused a flutter amongst local enthusiasts when it regularly appeared between Worcester and Hereford working Paddington services. Were they to take over these services on a regular basis? It later turned out this was just a convenient short round trip for Worcester driver traction training in readiness for dieselisation of the Fawley to Bromford Bridge, via Oxford and Worcester, oil tank trains. Worcester crews regularly worked these services although the depot's locomotives were not involved.

The story must now move on another year to September 1964, when the allocation was still falling but at a reduced rate from thirty-nine to thirty-three engines. The profile of the depot's workload was also changing with fresh turns replacing some of the losses. There was now very little steam-hauled passenger work, but main line freight duties had increased significantly for both Worcester's locomotives and crews. The depot now became a gathering ground for 5MT 'Grange' 4-6-0s on this increased freight work. Freight tripping was also still holding up in terms of service levels and steam operation. The depot's allocation now comprised four 5MT 'Hall' 4-6-0s, three 5MT 'Modified Hall' 4-6-0s, nine 5MT 'Grange' 4-6-0s, three 3MT 2251 0-6-0 tender engines, one 4MT 5101 2-6-2T, three 4MT 6100 2-6-2Ts, one 4MT 8100 2-6-2T, two 4F 9400 0-6-0PTs, six 3F 5700 0-6-0PTs and one 2F 1600 0-6-0PTs. The detailed allocation is once again set out in a separate table.

The summer 1964 timetable had seen 'Hymeks' return for the complete Paddington service, although the Kidderminster portion of 'The Cathedrals Express' still stubbornly arrived at Shrub Hill worked by a 5101 4MT 2-6-2 prairie tank. 'Halls' still had a passenger turn on a daily Birmingham Snow Hill commuter service from Evesham, via Stratford-on-Avon, with a balancing return working in the evening. They could also still sometimes appear between Worcester and Hereford on Paddington services. The Bromyard branch had closed to both passenger and freight services in September 1964. Long distance freight work was still, surprisingly, mainly steam hauled through the area. Worcester had in fact once again gained a number of extra longer distance freight duties from other depots. There were now an unprecedented ten daily freight main line locomotive turns and one standby duty at the depot. These were worked by its increased 5MT fleet of sixteen 'Halls', 'Modified Halls' and 'Granges', with the latter class in particular increasing in numbers. Locomotive condition was however variable and condition-led withdrawals continued throughout the period. Replacement engines, sometimes in little better condition, would regularly arrive. It was becoming a frustrating time both for footplate staff asked to work with locomotives in variable condition and equally for shed maintenance staff having to keep engines serviceable.

The depot still had over a year's life left, not finally closing to steam until the official cessation of scheduled steam working on the Western Region on 3 January 1966. That last operational year will be covered in the last chapter.

85A Worcester
Allocation 24 February 1962

'Castle' 7P 4-6-0	75000 4MT 4-6-0	5101 4MT 2-6-2T
5099 *Compton Castle*	75005	4113
7002 *Devizes Castle*	75025	4124
7005 *Sir Edward Elgar*	Total: 2	Total: 2
7007 *Great Western*		
7009 *Athelney Castle*	5205 8F 2-8-0T	8100 4MT 2-6-2T
7011 *Banbury Castle*	5205	8106
7013 *Bristol Castle*	5226	8107
7023 *Penrice Castle*	5245	Total: 2
7027 *Thornbury Castle*	Total: 3	
Total: 9		9400 4F 0-6-0PT
	4300 4MT 2-6-0	8415
'Hall' 5MT 4-6-0	5358	8480
4907 *Broughton Hall*	6368	9401
4963 *Rignall Hall*	6375	9486
5930 *Hannington Hall*	6387	9490
5944 *Ickenham Hall*	7315	Total: 5
5980 *Dingley Hall*	7338	
6947 *Helmingham Hall*	Total: 6	5700 3F 0-6-0PT
6948 *Holbrooke Hall*		3725
6951 *Impney Hall*	5600 5MT 0-6-2T	4613
Total: 8	5614 (stored)	4628
	6670 (stored)	4664
'Modified Hall' 5MT 4-6-0	Total: 2	4680
6984 *Owsden Hall*		Total: 5
6989 *Wightwick Hall*	2251 3MT 0-6-0	
6992 *Arborfield Hall*	2234	1600 2F 0-6-0PT
7920 *Coney Hall*	2246	1639
7928 *Wolf Hall*	3207	1661
Total: 5	Total: 3	Total: 2
'Grange' 5MT 4-6-0	78000 2MT 2-6-0	**Total Steam:** 61
6806 *Blackwell Grange*	78001	(inc. 2 stored)
6807 *Birchwood Grange*	78009	
6817 *Gwenddwr Grange*	Total: 2	
6856 *Stowe Grange*		
6877 *Llanfair Grange*		
Total: 5		

85A Worcester
Allocation 26 October 1963

'Castle' 7P 4-6-0	**75000 4MT 4-6-0**	**8100 4MT 2-6-2T**
7000 *Viscount Portal*	75005	8104
7002 *Devizes Castle*	75025	8106
7005 *Sir Edward Elgar*	Total: 2	Total: 2
7023 *Penrice Castle* (stored)		
7025 *Sudeley Castle*	**5205 8F 2-8-0T**	**9400 4F 0-6-0PT**
Total: 5	5205	8415
	5226	9490
'Hall' 5MT 4-6-0	5245	Total: 2
6948 *Holbrooke Hall*	Total: 3	
Total: 1		**5700 3F 0-6-0PT**
	2251 3MT 0-6-0	3725
'Modified Hall' 5MT 4-6-0	2222	4613
6992 *Arborfield Hall*	2232	4628
7920 *Coney Hall*	2246	4664
7926 *Willey Hall*	Total: 3	4680
7928 *Wolf Hall*		8793
Total: 4	**78000 2MT 2-6-0**	Total: 6
	78001	
	Total: 1	**1600 2F 0-6-0PT**
'Grange' 5MT 4-6-0		1639
6806 *Blackwell Grange*	**5101 4MT 2-6-2T**	1661
6807 *Birchwood Grange*	4113	Total: 2
6817 *Gwenddwr Grange*	5152	
6856 *Stowe Grange*	Total: 2	**Total Steam:** 39
6877 *Llanfair Grange*		(inc. 1 stored)
Total: 5	**6100 4MT 2-6-2T**	
	6155	
	Total: 1	

85A Worcester
Allocation 28 September 1964

'Hall' 5MT 4-6-0	2251 3MT 0-6-0	9400 4F 0-6-0PT
4903 *Astley Hall*	2222	8415
4919 *Donnington Hall*	2244	9490
5962 *Wantage Hall*	2253	Total: 2
6958 *Oxburgh Hall*	Total: 3	
Total: 4		5700 3F 0-6-0PT
	5101 4MT 2-6-2T	3682
'Modified Hall' 5MT 4-6-0	4113	3725
6995 *Benthall Hall*	Total: 1	4613
7920 *Coney Hall*		4664
7928 *Wolf Hall*	6100 4MT 2-6-2T	4680
Total: 3	6147	8793
	6155	Total: 6
'Grange' 5MT 4-6-0	6169	
6806 *Blackwell Grange*	Total: 3	1600 2F 0-6-0PT
6813 *Eastbury Grange*		1639
6817 *Gwenddwr Grange*	8100 4MT 2-6-2T	Total: 1
6819 *Highnam Grange*	8104	
6836 *Estevarney Grange*	Total: 1	**Total Steam: 33**
6848 *Toddington Grange*		
6856 *Stowe Grange*		
6877 *Llanfair Grange*		
6878 *Longford Grange*		
Total: 9		

Worcester's Engines and their Duties

Moving on, we will now look in greater detail at the principal classes of locomotive and their respective duties. The depot's flagship was undoubtedly the express passenger 7P 'Castle' 4-6-0s, supported by a strong allocation of mixed traffic 5MT 'Hall', 'Modified Hall' and 'Grange' 4-6-0s. It was also well populated with a middle order of 4MT prairie tanks and smaller tender locomotives for local passenger and freight trip work. Finally, there was the usual selection of pannier tanks to be found at most ex-GWR depots.

Collett 7P Castle 4-6-0s

No 7004 *Eastnor Castle* at Worcester on 17 February 1962 looking in fine external condition, just as Worcester's railwaymen and enthusiasts liked to remember their 'Castles'. Built in June 1946, it was a Worcester engine from July 1960 until September 1963 transfer to Reading. JOHN GOSS

Worcester 'Castles' – Locomotive Allocation
January 1960

4088 *Dartmouth Castle*	5071 *Spitfire*
4089 *Donnington Castle*	5081 *Lockheed Hudson*
5037 *Monmouth Castle*	7002 *Devizes Castle*
5039 *Rhuddlan Castle*	7005 *Sir Edward Elgar*
5042 *Winchester Castle*	7007 *Great Western*
	Total: 10

Worcester always took great pride in the condition of its relatively small but important 'Castle' class allocation. Worcester 'Castles' gained a reputation for their fine external condition. This was maintained well into the early 1960s, at a time when larger big city depot standards were falling and dieselisation, which would come comparatively late to Worcester, was taking its toll. The 'Castles' and their Paddington services are without question central to the Worcester story. They have been given their own discrete chapter later on, when a closer look will be taken at the best remembered fleet members and the services they worked.

5MT Halls, Modified Halls and Grange 4-6-0s

Collett's 1928 designed 'Halls' and the later 1944 Hawksworth 'Modified Halls' were to the untrained eye often regarded as a single interchangeable class of locomotives. In practice, 'Modified Halls' were particularly well regarded at passenger depots where they were seen as superior to the original 'Halls' for secondary cross-country passenger duties in particular. Worcester had a small select allocation and, whilst also to be found on freight work, several depot favourites were in turn identified and nurtured to stand in at short notice for 'Castles' on Worcester to Paddington journey legs. Indeed talking to retired Worcester footplate staff, the 'Modified Halls' were seen as particularly well

suited to the undulating, relatively frequent stopping pattern of the London route to Oxford. They were also capable of a good turn of speed over the final racetrack into Paddington assisted by the moderate loading of most of these services.

There were five 'Modified Halls' at the depot in January 1960 and this number would be maintained for the next three years. The allocation dropped to four in February 1963 and again to three in April 1964. There was a minor resurgence in December 1964 when it increased to six, although by now they would have been in variable condition and integrated with the 'Halls' and 'Granges' on main line freight work. There were several well-remembered depot time servers; in particular Nos 7920 *Coney Hall* from February 1951 to June 1965 withdrawal and 7928 *Wolf Hall* from newly built in October 1950 to March 1965 withdrawal. The last 'Modified Hall' left the depot in July 1965, just five months before depot closure.

By contrast, the fortunes of original 'Hall' 4-6-0s fluctuated over the years according to the amount of long distance freight work allocated at the time. They also shared the secondary passenger work in the early 1960s, including the daily 5.40pm Hereford to Worcester stopping service. This was a steam-hauled oddity amongst otherwise largely DMU dominated secondary services between Hereford and Worcester. It remained stubbornly steam-hauled until service withdrawal in May 1964.

The following 6.05pm Hereford to Paddington service was then retimed earlier and rather unsatisfactorily called at most local stations to Worcester. Another regular 'Hall' turn was the 8am Evesham to Birmingham Snow Hill, via Stratford-upon-Avon. It returned with the 5.45pm Birmingham Snow Hill to Evesham, via the same route. There were also regular 'Hall' round trips between Worcester and Hereford with Paddington portion services. The depot's 'Granges' although all diagrammed on freight work were in practice regarded as interchangeable on these secondary passenger turns.

There were nine 'Halls' on the allocation in January 1960 and until May 1961, after which numbers fluctuated between five and nine until collapsing to one or two from September 1962 onwards. There were no original 'Halls' allocated between November 1963 and June 1964, with 'Modified Halls' and 'Granges' dominating their previous work. Several then re-appeared and soldiered on until the last one left in July 1965. Due to the regular fluctuations in their fortunes over the years the 'Halls', unlike their 'Modified Hall' cousins, were a transient bunch with no long term depot time servers.

Collett's 5MT 'Grange' 4-6-0s were highly successful and well regarded mixed traffic engines and had the Second World War and then rail nationalisation not intervened, with the focus moving to the development of the BR Standard engine classes, the GWR would have continued building significantly more of this versatile eighty engines class.

Worcester had five 'Granges' in January 1960 and whilst their numbers briefly reduced they were back up to five by July 1961. Whilst individual engines changed, five in number was consistently maintained for the next three years until June 1964, when it almost doubled to nine locomotives. Previously, they had four long distance freight diagrams for the five engines allocated. This now increased to seven freight diagrams for the enhanced nine engines allocation. Interestingly, by June 1964 the one 'Hall' and two 'Modified Halls' remaining at the depot had just two passenger turns with all the scheduled freight work transferred to the 'Granges'. In the final two years of the depot's life the latter would become the dominant mixed traffic class at the depot.

There were two exceptionally long time serving engines; No 6807 *Birchwood Grange* from new in September 1936 until December 1963 withdrawal and No 6877 *Llanfair Grange* from new in May 1939 until March 1965 withdrawal. Equally worthy of mention is No 6851 *Hurst Grange* from new in December 1937 until transferred to Llanelly in July 1960.

Whilst diagrammed for the depot's freight work, the 'Granges' were as previously mentioned interchangeable with the 'Halls' and would regularly appear on secondary passenger work. Class 5 mixed traffic engines were the true jack of all trades on all the former company lines; be they ex-LMS Black 5s, ex-LNER B1s or here on former GWR territory, the 'Halls' and 'Granges'. Always ready to take on any mixed traffic work that could be thrown at them, typically No 6856 *Stowe Grange* worked a Worcester to Weston-Super-Mare passenger excursion on 23 July 1963 and the same again the following day. Clearly borrowed by Oxley when on a weekend freight layover, Worcester's No 6848 *Toddington Grange* handled a Wolverhampton Low Level to Bristol, via Stratford-upon-Avon, relief holiday express on Saturday 25 July 1964. The previous Saturday, Oxley similarly used Worcester's No 6813 *Eastbury Grange* for the 10.42am Wolverhampton Low Level to Margate and Sandwich, via Oxford and Guildford, holiday train. Not to be outdone, Oxford shed on Saturday 18 July 1964 used Worcester's No 7920 *Coney Hall*, whilst on a layover there, to work the 9.28am Bournemouth West to Manchester and Liverpool probably as far as Wolverhampton Low Level. No doubt these wanderers would eventually find their way back to Worcester, although this may have not been as prompt as would have been liked.

5.40pm Hereford to Worcester Shrub Hill – Author's Locomotive Sightings Diagrammed Worcester 'Hall' Mondays to Fridays, Hereford 'Hall' on Saturdays

75005 85A 5.40pm Hereford–Worcester SH, Hereford 13.3.63
6948 85A 5.40pm Hereford–Worcester SH, Hereford 15.5.63
6817 85A 5.40pm Hereford–Worcester SH, Hereford 24.5.63
44663 21A 5.40pm Hereford–Worcester SH, Hereford 30.5.63
6807 85A 5.40pm Hereford–Worcester SH, Hereford 4.6.63
6877 85A 5.40pm Hereford–Worcester SH, Hereford 6.6.63
7926 85A 5.40pm Hereford–Worcester SH, Hereford 11.6.63
6806 85A 5.40pm Hereford–Worcester SH, Hereford 13.6.63
7315 87F 5.40pm Hereford–Worcester SH, Hereford Sat 22.6.63
7928 85A 5.40pm Hereford–Worcester SH, Hereford 25.6.63
5998 86C 5.40pm Hereford–Worcester SH, Hereford Sat 29.6.63
7805 84E 5.40pm Hereford–Worcester SH, Hereford 4.7.63
75005 85A 5.40pm Hereford–Worcester SH, Hereford 8.7.63
6806 85A 5.40pm Hereford–Worcester SH, Hereford 9.7.63
6948 85A 5.40pm Hereford–Worcester SH, Hereford 10.7.63
6806 85A 5.40pm Hereford–Worcester SH, Hereford 11.7.63
7005 85A 5.40pm Hereford–Worcester SH, Hereford 20.9.63
6806 85A 5.40pm Hereford–Worcester SH, Hereford 24.9.63
7926 85A 5.40pm Hereford–Worcester SH, Hereford 21.10.63
6877 85A 5.40pm Hereford–Worcester SH, Hereford 22.10.63
6992 85A 5.40pm Hereford–Worcester SH, Hereford 19.11.63
6935 82E 5.40pm Hereford–Worcester SH, Hereford 19.1.63
6877 85A 5.40pm Hereford–Worcester SH, Hereford 20.2.64
6806 85A 5.40pm Hereford–Worcester SH, Hereford 5.3.64
7023 85A 5.40pm Hereford–Worcester SH, Hereford 7.4.64
6877 85A 5.40pm Hereford–Worcester SH, Hereford 23.4.64
7928 85A 5.40pm Hereford–Worcester SH, Hereford 24.4.64
7005 85A 5.40pm Hereford–Worcester SH, Hereford 27.4.64
7928 85A 5.40pm Hereford–Worcester SH, Hereford 24.4.64
4107 86C 5.40pm Hereford–Worcester SH, Hereford Sat 25.4.64
7928 85A 5.40pm Hereford–Worcester SH, Hereford 26.5.64
7928 85A 5.40pm Hereford–Worcester SH, Hereford 28.5.64

No 6992 *Arborfield Hall* departs Hereford with the early morning four coaches 6.20am to Paddington. The train will be made up to a full set of stock at Worcester Shrub Hill. Few are around to witness this early morning departure and the train was rarely recorded by enthusiasts. This 'Modified Hall' was released to traffic in November 1948 and was a Worcester engine from August 1959 until June 1964 withdrawal. DAVE WALDREN

No 7920 *Coney Hall* confidently stretches its legs through Norton Halt with a Hereford to Paddington service in spring 1962. The depot entrusted their best 'Modified Halls' with these services when a 'Castle' was not available and they performed well over the undulating Cotswolds route. Released to traffic in September 1950, *Coney Hall* was Worcester based for almost all its working life from February 1951 to June 1965 withdrawal. F.A. HAYNES

No 7928 *Wolf Hall* in fine external condition ready for its next turn of duty at Worcester on 9 September 1962. The ultimate single depot engine, it spent its whole working life at Worcester from new in October 1950 to March 1965 withdrawal. C.M. & J.M. Bentley

No 5980 *Dingley Hall.* This Worcester 'Hall' is on Shrewsbury shed around December 1958. In typically poor external condition, it would have arrived on an inwards freight working. Built in September 1938 and just transferred in from Gloucester in November 1958, it would have two spells at Worcester until June 1959 and from October 1961 to March 1962. Gordon Coltas Trust

No 5996 *Mytton Hall* 'in first rate external condition' is ready to come off shed in the hands of Worcester driver Charlie Huntley. A June 1940 build, the engine was based at Worcester from October 1959 to July 1961 and November to December 1961. DAVE WALDREN

No 6947 *Helmingham Hall* with passenger stock on the centre road at Hereford station around 1958. A wartime build in December 1942, it was already Worcester based on 1 January 1948 until September 1962 transfer to Gloucester. ANDREW SMITH COLLECTION

No 6817 *Gwenddwr Grange* in pristine newly re-painted condition, prominently displaying its Worcester shed plate, outside Swindon Works on 23 September 1962. A Heavy Intermediate overhaul had been undertaken and it would be released back to its home depot on 1 October. Built in December 1936, the engine was based at Worcester from July 1961 to April 1965 withdrawal. GERALD T. ROBINSON

No 6819 *Highnam Grange* in typical grimy freight working condition far from home with a goods train south of Wrexham on 2 September 1964. Released to traffic in December 1936, it was transferred to Worcester from Pontypool Road in June 1964 and remained at the depot until November 1965 withdrawal. It had last received a Heavy Intermediate overhaul at Swindon Works in November 1963. MANCHESTER LOCOMOTIVE SOCIETY

No 6820 *Kingstone Grange* has a rare moment of glory climbing Campden Bank with the 8am Hereford to Paddington 'The Cathedrals Express' around 1960. It would have taken over at Worcester Shrub Hill; a late replacement for a failed Worcester 'Castle'. Built in January 1937, it was a Worcester engine from October 1957 to April 1961. F.A. HAYNES

No 6848 *Toddington Grange* pauses at Basingstoke with a Summer Saturday holiday express from Wolverhampton Low Level to the South Coast on 4 July 1964. The 'Granges' were versatile engines quite capable of working express passenger cross country services. Almost certainly an Oxley turn, the depot had borrowed the Worcester engine whilst on layover there from an inwards freight working. Built in October 1937, it was Worcester based from January 1964 to November 1965 transfer to Oxford. C.M. & J.M. BENTLEY

No 6877 *Llanfair Grange* alongside the coaling hoist at Worcester in July 1963. Released to traffic in April 1939, it was a long serving Worcester engine based there from new, until March 1965 withdrawal. Railphotoprints

BR Standard 4MT 75000 4-6-0s

These were Worcester's only flirtation with BR Standard mixed traffic engines, these having a small but long-standing role at the depot. Nos 75023 and 75025 were first to arrive in November 1957. Whilst individual engines changed, the allocation remained at two through to January 1964, except for two minor periods when it dropped to a single engine. Nos 75005

and 75025 ended the classes' first spell at the depot when transferred to Gloucester Horton Road in January 1964.

The 75000s were regarded as interchangeable on most 'Hall' and 'Grange' duties and might be found covering freight work or secondary passenger services. No 75005 was noted on 13 March and 8 July 1963 working the 5.40pm Hereford to Worcester local passenger service.

WORCESTER'S ENGINES AND THEIR DUTIES • 59

Throughout 1963, one of the then pair was officially documented to be a Honeybourne out-based banking engine, although photographic evidence suggests this duty was more commonly entrusted at the time to 3MT 2251 0-6-0s. The second 75000 was the nominated spare at Worcester. The two longest time servers were No 75005 from January 1961 to January 1964 and No 75025 in three separate spells from November 1957 to August 1960,

October 1960 to January 1964 and May to December 1965.

After an eighteen month gap, Nos 75008, 75022 and 75025 appeared from Exmouth Junction in May 1965, followed by Nos 75000, 75003 and 75005 from Yeovil Junction in June. This was part of a rather chaotic moving roundabout of surviving mixed traffic engines in the final months of Western Region in an attempt to maintain remaining steam commitments amongst an increasingly unserviceable fleet.

No 75000 passes through Birmingham Snow Hill with an up freight on 4 September 1965. Partially obscured is Tyseley's No 7915 *Mere Hall* on station pilot duty. Built in 1951, No 75000 was a late arrival at Worcester in June 1965. Six of the class had arrived during May and June from Exmouth Junction and Yeovil to bolster up the ailing Worcester mixed traffic fleet until depot closure at the end of the year. R.N. PRITCHARD

No 75003 terminating with an Oxford to Malvern Wells local service about 1960. Built in August 1951, it was amongst the first of a small allocation at Worcester. It arrived from Swindon in February 1958 and remained until January 1961 before returning with the cavalry from Yeovil in June 1965 until its October 1965 withdrawal. TIM FAREBROTHER

No 75022 pauses at Malvern Link with a down passenger service on 27 July 1965; by this date one of the very few remaining steam hauled passenger services. Entering service in December 1953, No 75022 had a short stay at Worcester from May to its December 1965 withdrawal. R.N. PRITCHARD

Churchward 4MT 4300 2-6-0s

These hard working but rather old-fashioned-looking engines were quite capable of handling long distance freight trains and at some depots worked longer distance branch line passenger services. They had once been a regular part of the Worcester scene, with ten or more being allocated there during the 1950s. However, decline set in from 1957 and there was just one left at Worcester in January 1960. Numbers did then rise to between five and seven for a while before another steady decline saw the class finally disappear from the depot in July 1962. Whilst they could and probably did in the early days handle main line freight work, they were latterly more likely to be found on freight tripping duties along the main lines around Worcester. Their patchy presence here is in contrast to their successful longer term usage at some other depots. Notably well into 1964 at Taunton they were the class of choice on branch passenger and freight services to Barnstaple and at Gloucester Horton Road to Hereford.

No 6368 has paused at Stoulton with a Honeybourne to Worcester freight trip and is about to shunt the yard around 1962. An October 1925 build, it was a Worcester engine from June to December 1959 and July 1960 to June 1962. F.A. HAYNES

No 6387 hurries along the centre road through Birmingham Snow Hill station on 14 August 1961. It may have worked in the morning Evesham to Birmingham Snow Hill, via Stratford-upon-Avon, commuter train or a freight service from the Worcester area. Entering traffic in September 1921, No 6387 was based at Worcester from December 1960 to June 1962 withdrawal. JOHN GOSS

Collett 8F 5205 2-8-0Ts

These heavy freight tank engines, designed specifically for South Wales colliery work, first appeared on the Worcester allocation in February 1960. This was coincidental with responsibility for the Ledbury sub-shed transferring from Hereford to Worcester, following the former's re-designation as a Newport Motive Power District depot. Along with the depot transfer came No 5243, followed by Nos 5245 and then 5226 from Bromsgrove. The latter was after an unsuccessful trial as a Lickey Incline banking engine. No 5243 soon moved on to Gloucester Horton Road in April 1960, leaving Nos 5226 and 5245 as the two regulars on the Worcester allocation. A third class member 'No 5205' appeared in January 1962 until all three left in January 1964.

One of the engines was out-based at Ledbury all week on banking duties, being sent out light engine from Worcester on Monday mornings and returning after the last train in the early hours of the following Sunday morning.

Three sets of footplate crews were based at Ledbury to cover this continuous banking turn. Whilst three 5205s were on the allocation, the workload was one Ledbury banking turn and one Worcester freight turn, with the third engine held spare. Following the re-allocation of the 5205s in January 1964, Ledbury banking duties were taken over by Collett 4MT 2-6-2 prairie tanks.

No 5205 approaches Stoulton with a lengthy Honeybourne to Worcester freight trip in 1963. This interestingly has two brake vans formed in the train's centre. Principally allocated to Worcester for Ledbury banking duties, the 5205 2-8-0s were sometimes used for local freight trips, although with an 8F power rating they were capable of more arduous tasks. F.A. HAYNES

No 5205 pulls powerfully away towards the left hand fork at Norton Junction with a Worcester to Cotswolds line freight trip on 9 May 1963. The link to Abbots Wood Junction and the ex-Midland railway Derby to Bristol route drops away to the right. This 1923 built engine was the first of Collett's modified class, with enlarged cylinders and detailed alterations, of Churchward's 1910 designed 4200 2-8-0Ts. It was based at Worcester from January 1962 to November 1963 withdrawal. BEN ASHWORTH

No 5245 on shed at Worcester in the 1960s. Released to traffic in November 1925, it was Worcester based from February 1960 to January 1964 transfer to Llanelly. It was a regular choice at Ledbury on banking duties. RAIL-ONLINE

Collett 3MT 2251 0-6-0s

These useful mixed traffic engines were a familiar sight around the Worcester area for many years. Mostly used on local freight trip work they were also the regular choice for Honeybourne banking duties. The class was also a popular choice for working weekend engineering trains and in winter the designated standby for snowplough duties. In January 1960, there were ten here, two of which were in store, although these would later be reinstated and transferred away. By July 1960, the allocation was down to six, reducing to three by August 1961 after which the numbers stabilised at three or four through to February 1965. The last two examples, Nos 2222 and 2244, were withdrawn in May 1965. The individual

engines involved were a transient bunch with no less than twenty different examples passing through the depot's hands between 1960 and 1965. The changes were mostly driven by condition-led withdrawals, with replacement engines in so-called better condition drafted in from other depots where they were surplus to requirements.

Typically, in February 1962 the 2251s' workload comprised two freight trips with a third engine held spare. They were most commonly used on freight trips over the Cotswolds line towards Evesham and Honeybourne, several being mixed diagrams that included part of the day on Honeybourne banking duties. They would prove to be much photographed whilst on the latter duties.

No 2222 on shed at Worcester on 20 September 1964. These versatile light mixed traffic engines were principally used in the Worcester area for freight tripping and Honeybourne banking duties. No 2222 was a wartime August 1940 build, based at Worcester from May 1962 until May 1965 withdrawal. It and No 2244, withdrawn together, were the last class members based at the depot. MANCHESTER LOCOMOTIVE SOCIETY

No 2232 brings a short Bromyard branch freight trip through Suckley. It was less common to find a 2251 class 0-6-0 on this turn, which was usually worked by a 5700 0-6-0PT. No 2232 entered service in October 1944, working at Worcester between March 1963 and September 1964 withdrawal. DAVID WILSON. ANDREW SMITH COLLECTION

No 2244 stabled outside Worcester Works with a ladder up against the boiler on 30 June 1965. An April 1945 build, it had been based at Worcester since September 1964 and had been withdrawn on 21 May 1965, a month prior to the photograph being taken. It was still a little surprisingly carrying its number plates. R.N. PRITCHARD

Collett 4MT 5101, 6100, 8100 and BR Standard 3MT 82000 2-6-2Ts

The three very similar Collett classes were treated as a single group in terms of Worcester's allocation and workload. The more numerous 5101 class dominated the allocation for much of the period. There were just two 8100s based at Worcester at any one time; the longest time server No 8106 already on the allocation on 1 January 1948 and remained there until December 1963 withdrawal. The 6100s, primarily built for London commuter work, were, after the latter's dieselisation, increasingly moved out to provincial depots where they tended to survive longer in service than the 5101s. Worcester received its first, No 6155, in September 1962 with eventually seven different

examples passing through the depot's hands. An average of three 6100 engines were based here at any one time.

There were seven of the more numerous 5101 class on the allocation in January 1960, although the numbers more typically averaged between three and five before dropping to two between October 1961 and June 1962. Numbers eventually settled at two from December 1963 through to their November 1965 demise. Some of the variations were due to balanced increases in the 6100 and 8100 allocations with which they shared common duties. The final 8100 class example No 8104 was withdrawn in December 1964, the last 5101 class members Nos 4113 and 4161 in November 1965 and the final 6100 class member No 6147 in readiness for depot closure on 31 December 1965.

No 4124 makes a station call at Hartlebury with a local passenger service for the Worcester area in the 1960s. A January 1938 build, it was based at Worcester from September 1958 to August 1964 withdrawal, except for a short October to December 1963 spell at Aberdare. PETER REEVES. MANCHESTER LOCOMOTIVE SOCIETY

At Worcester, the combined classes of prairie tanks were principally used for local passenger duties on the main lines into Worcester and increasingly on local freight trips towards Kidderminster and along the Cotswolds line. Typically, in January 1963, there was an allocation of seven prairie tanks working two daily local passenger and three local freight tripping turns. The local passenger work was however steadily lost to DMU operation. However, a single late afternoon Worcester-hauled local service on the Hereford line survived until the end of the summer 1964 timetable; although records of this still being steam-worked in practice exist well into 1965, as do that at times it would be worked by a Stourbridge Junction based prairie tank on a Worcester layover. The freight trip work proved more resilient, remaining steam-hauled almost to depot closure. During 1964, the Ledbury banking duties also passed from the 8F 5205 2-8-0s on their departure to a prairie tank turn. Ledbury closed as a depot in July 1964 although the single banking duty is shown as being worked out of Worcester as required until the end of December 1964.

Three BR Standard 3MT 82000 2-6-2Ts arrived at the shed in 1955. Two moved on to Wellington in September 1959, leaving just No 82008 as the 1960s dawned. This single engine shared local passenger duties with ex-GWR 4MT 2-6-2Ts until it moved on to Machynlleth in June 1961. Worcester, with a relatively modern ex-GWR locomotive fleet, never really had the need for many BR Standard locomotives.

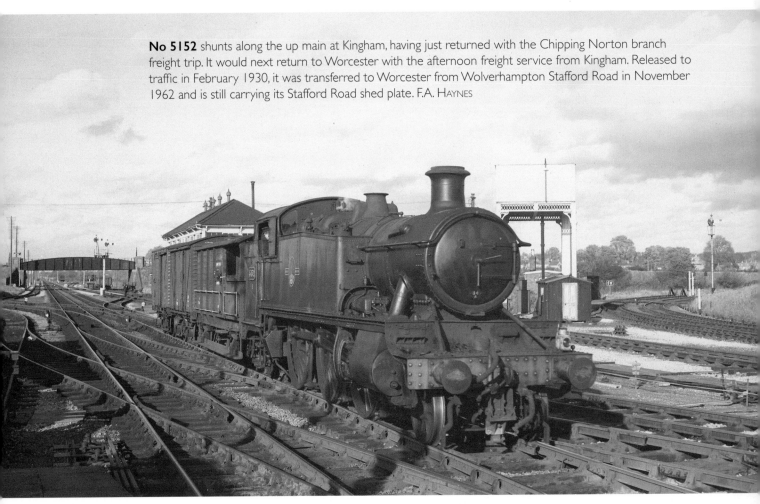

No 5152 shunts along the up main at Kingham, having just returned with the Chipping Norton branch freight trip. It would next return to Worcester with the afternoon freight service from Kingham. Released to traffic in February 1930, it was transferred to Worcester from Wolverhampton Stafford Road in November 1962 and is still carrying its Stafford Road shed plate. F.A. HAYNES

No 6140 on shed at Worcester in 1964. The 4MT 6100 2-6-2Ts were introduced for London commuter work, although examples found their way to the provinces particularly after their intended work was dieselised. No 6140, released to traffic in November 1932, had a relatively short stay at Worcester from January to July 1964 withdrawal. IAN CATLING

No 6147 outside Swindon Works awaiting release back to traffic on 26 April 1964. January 1933 built, it was officially transferred from Westbury to Worcester on 25 January 1964 but underwent a Heavy Casual overhaul at Swindon Works between 24 January and 1 May before heading for its new depot. It would prove a valuable acquisition, working until 31 December 1965 withdrawal coincidental with depot closure. IAN TURNBULL. RAIL PHOTOPRINTS

No 6155 resting beside Worcester shed on 17 May 1964. Entering service in March 1933, it reached Worcester from Westbury in September 1962, working from the depot until October 1965 withdrawal. ROY PALMER

No 8106. This small class of engines were rebuilds of earlier Churchward 5101 2-6-2Ts with higher boiler pressure and smaller wheels. No 8106 entered service in June 1939 and was already a Worcester resident on 1 January 1948 from where it worked until December 1963 withdrawal. Seen here at rest at Evesham on 7 June 1963; its crew probably taking a meal break whilst on a local freight trip along the Cotswolds line. DAVE WALDREN

No 8107 on shed at Worcester set against a dramatic sky on 17 February 1962 with the depot's steam crane No 43 loading spent locomotive ash in the background. No 8107 entered service in July 1939; arriving from Gloucester in July 1961 it would be withdrawn in May 1962. JOHN GOSS

No 82030 stands on empty stock on the through line at Worcester Shrub Hill on 31 May 1959. The depot had a brief flirtation with the 3MT BR Standard 82000 2-6-2Ts which were here regarded as interchangeable with the ex-GWR 4MT 2-6-2Ts. No 82030 was Swindon Works built in December 1954 and Worcester based from December 1955 until September 1959. It also had two brief monthly spells at Kidderminster during the final year. DAVE WALDREN

BR Standard 2MT 78000 2-6-0s

No 78001 on shed at Worcester on 17 December 1962. Released to traffic from Darlington Works in December 1952, it arrived at Worcester from Machynlleth in May 1954, working here until its January 1964 transfer to Gloucester. It was regularly to be found out-based at Kingham. JOHN GOSS

The 78000s were present at Worcester in small numbers from July 1953. They arrived to replace the last surviving light axle weight Dean Goods 2301 0-6-0s in the area. Those finally replaced were the aged 1895 built No 2458 and 1897 built No 2551 during 1953 and 1954. The 78000s were mainly used on local freight trip work; one always being out-based at Kingham. Duties included the axle weight restricted Moreton-in-Marsh to Shipton-on-Stour branch freight until branch closure in May 1960. The single Kingham duty was a little misleadingly recorded in the depot's diagram summary returns as a passenger turn. It did in fact have a minor local passenger element first thing in the morning, but the engine spent the rest of the day on freight trip and shunting duties. A second class member worked a further local freight trip duty from Worcester, whilst the third engine was a spare.

Nos 78001, 78008 and 78009 were resident at the depot in January 1960. The allocation gradually reduced with No 78008 leaving for Wolverhampton Stafford Road in January 1962 and Nos 78009 and 78001 for Gloucester Barnwood in March 1963 and January 1964 respectively. These reductions were a combination of reduced workload and Collett 3MT 2251s absorbing their duties.

Collett 3F 5700 and Hawksworth 4F 9400 0-6-0PTs

There were still 723 of the hard working and reliable 1929 designed Collett 3F 5700 pannier tanks around the system in 1960, being found at almost all ex-GWR main depots. Here at Worcester there were ten allocated in January 1960, but the number had halved to five by July 1961, due to the arrival during the previous year of an equivalent number of 204hp diesel mechanical (later class 03) shunting engines. These would cover four freight shunting turns in the Worcester area. The 5700s' numbers remained consistent for the next two years until increasing marginally to six in March 1963. After another steady year, the allocation peaked at seven in October 1964 before falling back to four by February 1965. Only a further one was lost before the final cull of the three remaining engines Nos 3682, 4680 and 9626 on the infamous 31 December 1965. The longest depot time server, amongst a number of familiar residents over the years, was No 3725 from September 1948 until January 1965 withdrawal.

In February 1962, the five engines' allocation had four daily diagrammed turns: one local passenger, one freight service and two shunting duties. The passenger turn was on the Bromyard branch and one of the shunting turns the Shrub Hill station passenger pilot. With the allocation now up to six, an extra freight trip turn was taken on in September 1963. Workload remained at this level until 5 September 1964, when the local passenger diagram was lost following the withdrawal of Bromyard branch services.

The Hawksworth 1947 designed 4F 9400 0-6-0PTs were a controversial large locomotive build which in retrospect were barely justifiable and certainly not in the numbers ordered. Only the first ten were built by the GWR in 1947, with the following 200 built to committed GWR orders after nationalisation between 1949 and 1956. The latter 200 engines, possibly partly for political reasons, were built by private locomotive builders Bagnalls at Stafford, Yorkshire Engine Company at Sheffield and Robert Stephenson and Hawthorn at Darlington. By the time the build was completed in 1956 diesel shunting engines were coming on stream in significant numbers and local freight work was reducing.

The practical outcome saw some engines being stored unallocated for some months after delivery from the private manufacturers. Others after initial allocation found themselves placed in store for many months followed by unseemly early withdrawals. Typically, Worcester had an inflated allocation in comparison with workloads. It fluctuated between ten and eleven during 1960, falling to eight that October and then steadily reducing to two by October 1962 after which the number stabilised until December 1964. The class disappeared from the depot in February 1965 until a single example returned from May to July 1965.

The eleven allocated engines in August 1960 had a ridiculously small four daily turns and four of the engines, Nos 8460, 8496, 9455 and 9480, were to be found in store at Kidderminster; a regular bolthole then for storing surplus Worcester engines. By February 1962, the depot's fleet of six 9400s had just one daily duty, although they did also provide spare cover for the depot's six 5700 0-6-0PTs. The single turn was still in place throughout 1963 and 1964, when records confirm it as the 11.05am Worcester Yard to Henwick and Malvern line freight trip. By the summer 1964 timetable, the turn included the by then Tuesdays and Fridays only Bromyard branch freight trip, although former Worcester staff remember 5700s being more usually provided on this service.

No 3615 on passenger station pilot duty at Worcester Shrub Hill on 31 July 1965 with driver Tommy Smith in charge. The freight yard pilots had been dieselised in 1960 but the passenger pilot was still a steam turn at this late date. No 3615 was released to traffic in March 1939; a relatively late arrival at Worcester from Neath in January 1965, it would only last until an October 1965 withdrawal. R.N. Pritchard

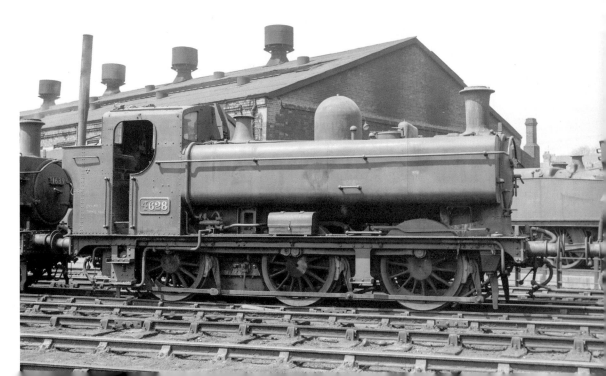

No 4628 resting on Worcester shed on 1 June 1963. It was an October 1942 wartime build, arriving at the depot from Gloucester in December 1960 and worked from there until May 1964 withdrawal. R.C. Riley. Transport Treasury

No 4664 being prepared at Worcester in April 1964. Young firemen Bill Adams and Brian Hodson chat whilst the latter trims an oil lamp. Meanwhile, driver Neville Hodson undertakes footplate preparation. No 4664 entered service in November 1943 and was already a Worcester engine on 1 January 1948. Apart from several monthly spells away at Kidderminster once and Gloucester twice, it would remain a Worcester engine until July 1965 withdrawal. TIM FAREBROTHER

No 4680 brings a local trip into the up loop between Rainbow Hill and Worcester Tunnel junctions. Rainbow Hill Junction signal box is in the background. The engine was June 1944 built and had two spells at Worcester from August to November 1957 and October 1961 to December 1965 withdrawal. RALPH WARD

No 8415 photographed against a rather dramatic sky at Worcester on 17 February 1962. The depot's generous early allocation soon diminished and despite their 4F power rating they were used here for nothing that couldn't easily have been handled by 3F 5700 0-6-0PTs. No 8415 was delivered new from private builder Bagnalls of Stafford to Tyseley in March 1950, transferring to Worcester July 1960. Two spells at Worcester followed from then until February 1965 and May to June 1965 withdrawal. JOHN GOSS

Hawksworth 2F 1600 0-6-0PTs

These smaller pannier tanks had the typical looks of a GWR design, although all seventy engines were delivered after nationalisation between 1949 and 1955; the Swindon design pre-dating the development of BR standard locomotive classes. Despite some having relatively short service lives, there was in this case good justification for the build. They were intended to fill an important gap in the Western Region's small light axle weight tank engine fleet. The elderly tank engines they would replace had mainly survived where restricted access routes and sidings barred the otherwise all conquering 5700 class 0-6-0PTs being used. Still at work at rail nationalisation in 1948 were a surprising number of 1897 William Dean designed light axle weight 2021 2F class tank engines. Despite having been rebuilt as pannier tanks over the years, they were long overdue replacement and as 1600s were delivered these were rapidly withdrawn.

In January 1960, Worcester had two 2F 0-6-0PT class members, Nos 1629 and 1661, to cover a single specialised turn known as the Vinegar branch trip, whilst the second engine was held spare.

This trip also acted as the shed pilot for berthing locomotive coaling wagons. It also shunted several traffic sidings within the shed complex and serviced a coal delivery depot accessed from the shed site. The Vinegar branch started from the shed yard, immediately crossing the Shrub Hill station to Rainbow Hill Junction side of the Worcester triangle on a flat crossing. It then descended rapidly over an ungated public road crossing to serve Hill Evans & Co. vinegar distillers and several other private sidings. The last branch train ran on 5 June 1964 hauled by No 1639.

A two engine allocation was consistently maintained over the years up to July 1964, although the individual engines changed as condition led withdrawals occurred. The end came with the withdrawal of No 1661 in July 1964, followed by No 1639 that October. The longest serving resident and seemingly most photographed was No 1661. It had arrived from Kidderminster in November 1957 and worked until July 1964 withdrawal. It was fitted with a spark arrester chimney throughout its Worcester time. This actually had been a requirement of its former Kidderminster duties and was not necessary for the Vinegar branch working.

No 2034 was an ex-GWR Dean 2021 class 0-6-0, released to traffic in November 1897 from Wolverhampton Works and later rebuilt as a pannier tank. It was a Worcester engine from May 1951 to April 1954, where it performed duties later undertaken by the 1600 class 0-6-0PTs. It was withdrawn from Kidderminster in September 1955 and sold to the National Coal Board. Pictured here off its wheels but still carrying its original cab-side number plate at Hafodyrynys Colliery, Monmouthshire, on 31 May 1962. My school railway society members surround this rare find from a bygone age. I am the young teenager in a dark blazer. JOHN GOSS

No 1629 traverses Worcester's Shrub Hill Road's open crossing with a Vinegar Branch freight trip on 27 May 1958; fireman Mick Fenson is standing on the footplate. No 1629 entered service in September 1950 working from Worcester between September 1953 and June 1960 withdrawal when it was replaced by No 1647 from Gloucester Horton Road. NEVILL STEAD COLLECTION. TRANSPORT TREASURY

Shrub Hill Road Crossing on the Vinegar branch featured unusual lower quadrant signals for controlling road traffic over the crossing. That date is 1 April 1965 and the branch has been closed for almost a year. JOHN RUMSEY. STEVE BARTLETT COLLECTION

No 1661 with spark arrester chimney on a short Vinegar Branch freight trip having just passed the open road crossing. The engine is carrying an express passenger train head-code. JOHN MUDGE

No 1639, looking surprisingly clean, takes water on shed at Worcester. The image is undated, but the locomotive underwent a Heavy General overhaul at Wolverhampton Works in February 1962 which helps to date the photo. No 1639 was allocated newly built to Lydney for Forest of Dean work in March 1951, moving on to Worcester in February 1961 until October 1964 withdrawal. DAVE WALDREN

No 1661 complete with spark arrester chimney at Worcester in this undated scene. Allocated newly built to Kidderminster in March 1955, it moved to Worcester in November 1957. It was one of the longest serving and most photographed of the Worcester 1600s, not being withdrawn from there until July 1964 just after Vinegar branch closure. A rare visitor alongside is Hawksworth 6MT 4-6-0 No 1011 *County of Chester*, Bristol-based for most of its working life. TONY HOSKINS. ANDREW SMITH COLLECTION

Monthly Summary of Depot Locomotive Workload

The depot was required each four week ending to submit a summary of its daily diagram workload by class of locomotive and type of duties. This was submitted to the District office. It in turn collated this into a district return and submitted it to Western Region headquarters. Some of the collated regional returns have survived in the BR records at the National Archives Kew for the period January 1963 to May 1965. A copy of one earlier return for February 1962 has also been found in my late-father's papers.

There were however compilation quirks that need to be understood for correct interpretation of the figures.

Our Worcester compiler sometimes included the depot's sub-shed work within the main shed return and at other times listed them separately. These inconsistencies are usually easy to spot. The return only includes full week diagrams and excludes single day variations such as Saturday or Sunday only work. When a diagram contained mixed passenger and freight duties it was at the whim of the compiler under which heading the diagram was listed. Parcels train work was not separately defined and would be included within the passenger category. A selection of the four weekly returns is included here, giving a rare insight into the overall depot workload at any one time.

Locomotive Weekday Turns Summary – Worcester Shed
Four Weeks Ending 24 February 1962

Engine Class	Passgr. & Parcels	Freight	Shunt	Banking	Specials	Total Turns	Engines Allocated
'Castle' 7P 4-6-0	6					6	9
'Hall' 5MT 4-6-0	1	7			1	9	13
'Grange' 5MT 4-6-0		3				3	5
'75000' 4MT 4-6-0		1				1	2
'4300' 4MT 2-6-0		4				4	5
'2251' 3MT 0-6-0		2				2	3
'78000' 2MT 2-6-0		1				1	1
'5205' 8F 2-8-0T		1				1	2
'5101'* 4MT 2-6-2T	1	2				3	4
'9400' 4F 0-6-0PT		1				1	6
'5700' 3F 0-6-0PT	1	1	2			4	5
'1600' 2F 0-6-0PT			1			1	2
Total Steam	**9**	**23**	**3**		**1**	**36**	**58**
*including '6100s' & '8100s'							
Diesel 204hp			4			4	5
Kingham Sub-shed							
'78000' 2MT 2-6-0	1					1	1
Ledbury Sub-shed							
'5205' 8F 2-8-0T				1		1	1
Grand Total Steam	**10**	**23**	**3**	**1**	**1**	**38**	**60**

Note: No separate official allocation Honeybourne

Locomotive Weekday Turns Summary – Worcester Shed
Four Weeks Ending 26 January 1963

Engine Class	Passgr. & Parcels	Freight	Shunt	Banking	Specials	Total Turns	Engines Allocated
'Castle' 7P 4-6-0	6					6	9
'Hall' 5MT 4-6-0	2	3				5	5
'Grange' 5MT 4-6-0		2			1	3	5
'75000' 4MT 4-6-0						0	1
'2251' 3MT 0-6-0		2				2	3
'78000' 2MT 2-6-0		2				2	2
'5205' 8F 2-8-0T		1				1	2
'5101'* 4MT 2-6-2T	2	3				5	7
'9400' 4F 0-6-0PT		1				1	2
'5700' 3F 0-6-0PT	1		2.5			3.5	5
'1600' 2F 0-6-0PT			1			1	2
Total Steam	**11**	**14**	**3.5**		**1**	**29.5**	**43**
*including '6100s' & '8100s'							
Diesel 204hp			4			4	5
Honeybourne Sub-shed							
'75000' 4MT 4-6-0				1		1	1
Ledbury Sub-shed							
'5205' 8F 2-8-0T				1		1	1
Grand Total Steam	**11**	**14**	**3.5**	**2**	**1**	**31.5**	**45**

Locomotive Weekday Turns Summary – Worcester Shed
Four Weeks Ending 28 December 1963

Engine Class	Passgr. & Parcels	Freight	Shunt	Banking	Specials	Total Turns	Engines Allocated
'Castle' 7P 4-6-0	2					2	5
'Hall' 5MT 4-6-0	2				1	3	4
'Grange' 5MT 4-6-0		4				4	5
'75000' 4MT 4-6-0						0	0
'2251' 3MT 0-6-0		2				2	3
'78000' 2MT 2-6-0		1				1	1
'5205' 8F 2-8-0T		1				1	2
'5101'* 4MT 2-6-2T	1	2				3	4
'9400' 4F 0-6-0PT		1				1	2
'5700' 3F 0-6-0PT	1	2	2.5			5.5	6
'1600' 2F 0-6-0PT		1				1	2
Total Steam	**6**	**13**	**3.5**		**1**	**23.5**	**34**
*including '6100s' & '8100s'							
Diesel 204hp			4			4	5
Honeybourne Sub-shed							
'75000' 4MT 4-6-0				1.5		1.5	2
Ledbury Sub-shed							
'5205' 8F 2-8-0T				1		1	1
Grand Total Steam	**6**	**13**	**3.5**	**2.5**	**1**	**26**	**37**

Locomotive Weekday Turns Summary – Worcester Shed
Four Weeks Ending 3 October 1964

Engine Class	Passgr. & Parcels	Freight	Shunt	Banking	Specials	Total Turns	Engines Allocated
'Castle' 7P 4-6-0						0	0
'Hall' 5MT 4-6-0	2	3			1	6	7
'Grange' 5MT 4-6-0		7				7	9
'2251' 3MT 0-6-0		1				1	2
'5101'* 4MT 2-6-2T		3				3	4
'9400' 4F 0-6-0PT		1				1	2
'5700' 3F 0-6-0PT		2	2			4	6
'1600' 2F 0-6-0PT			1			1	1
Total Steam	**2**	**17**	**3**		**1**	**23**	**31**
*including '6100s' & '8100s'							
Diesel 204hp			4			4	5
Honeybourne Sub-shed							
'2251' 3MT 0-6-0				1		1	1
Ledbury Sub-shed							
'5101' 4MT 2-6-2T				1		1	1
Grand Total Steam	**2**	**17**	**3**	**2**	**1**	**25**	**33**

Worcester
Locomotive Works

Worcester Works' rather cramped Erecting Shop in April 1964 with ex-GWR 5MT mixed traffic 4-6-0s prominently in view. Whilst Worcester engines dominated it also often hosted engines from further afield. TIM FAREBROTHER

Worcester Locomotive Works, also locally known as 'The Factory', was situated immediately opposite the engine shed on the right hand side of the main line heading north from Shrub Hill towards Worcester Tunnel Junction. It was the principal heavy maintenance and repair facility for the Worcester Motive Power District and was responsible for all major mileage examinations and heavy repairs. This left the District's locomotive sheds to concentrate on lesser mileage examinations and basic running repairs. The works also undertook heavy lifting, enabling driving wheels removal and access to locomotive underparts when this was not available at home depots. It also undertook repairs on engines from distant sheds that had failed in traffic in the Worcester area or were occasionally specifically sent from further afield for attention.

The locomotive works, despite its proximity and very similar work skills to the motive power depot, was not under the Shed Master's control but reported direct to the District Running & Maintenance Office. Edgar Richardson was in charge at the works with the rather understated job title of Locomotive Factory Foreman. On his retirement in 1961, he was succeeded by works Chargeman and principal assistant Don Green.

The locomotive works was a great survivor over the years, having passed through the ownership of four different railway companies. It had also seen a number of major organisational and role changes, several of which threatened its closure. It would however survive until the end of Western Region steam operations in 1965, playing an essential role in that final year keeping an increasingly ailing fleet operational. It also at that time undertook work on a number of locomotives passing into private preservation.

The works' origins go back to the Oxford, Worcester and Wolverhampton Railway; Worcester being one of its centres of operations. In 1860 the company joined with the Newport, Abergavenny and Hereford Railway, the Worcester and Hereford Railway and the Coleford, Monmouth, Usk and Pontypool Railway to form the West Midlands Railway. The latter in turn sought early amalgamation with the Great Western Railway. This took place in August 1863 under whose control the works remained until rail nationalisation in 1948.

In GWR days, the locomotive works was part of the all-embracing Chief Mechanical Engineer's department at Swindon. This oversaw all aspects of locomotive and carriage and wagon work, including construction, overhaul, maintenance and the provision of motive power for operating department use. However, in 1949, following rail nationalisation the previous year, this vast empire was split three ways. This created a separate Mechanical and Electrical Engineer's department responsible for locomotive workshops and outdoor machinery, a Carriage and Wagon Engineer's department with similar discrete responsibilities and a Motive Power Superintendent's department responsible for motive power depots, shed and footplate staff. This saw Worcester's engine shed and works separate under different chains of command, with Swindon independently determining the role and allocation of work to the locomotive works. These regional facilities were headed by the larger main works at Swindon, Wolverhampton and Caerphilly, but also included such smaller workshops as those at Barry, Oswestry, Newton Abbot and Worcester. In 1951, storm clouds gathered as it was decided there was workshop over capacity and rationalisation was proposed. This included the complete closure of Worcester's locomotive works, although the adjacent carriage and wagon workshop was to remain open. Worcester's then District Motive Power Superintendent, Bill Blakesley, was responsible for the area's motive power depots. He realised that significant problems would be encountered if the support of the local locomotive works was lost. He therefore made a formal proposal to take the works into his organisation. This would see a structured division of maintenance and repair work, with Worcester Works concentrating on the District's heavy maintenance examinations and repairs, leaving the depots to focus on light maintenance and running repairs. This followed ex-LMS practice where Bill Blakesley had his origins and was now being more widely adopted elsewhere. The proposal was accepted and Worcester Works settled down into a role that would last until closure. Brian Penny, who started at Worcester as an apprentice fitter and later occupied a number of senior management maintenance roles within the Western Region, recalls the Oswestry Works Manager visited Worcester to discuss the recently changed arrangements with a view to a similar role change in the Cambrian Motive Power District.

The locomotive works had a comparatively small capacity considering the important role it undertook. Under the same roof was a cramped Erecting Shop where the locomotives stood in line. Behind this through a partition wall was the Fitting Shop where staff worked on machines and lathes refurbishing locomotive parts for re-fitting. Beyond this under the same roof was the Blacksmiths Shop, which also undertook work for the Carriage and Wagon department. By the 1960s, what had once been steam belt driven machinery was now electrically operated. Within the Fitting Shop was a belt driven locomotive wheel profiling machine that could handle up to six foot driving wheels. Anything larger, as for instance on the 'Castles', had to be sent to Swindon Works. It is said this wheel profiling machine originated from the Midland and South Western Junction Railway's locomotive works at Cirencester. Following Worcester Works' closure it was purchased by the then fledgling Dart Valley Railway for their locomotive maintenance facility.

Access to the Erecting Shop was by means of an electric motor powered traverser, illustrated in the photographs that follow. This traverser was moved across the front of the Erecting Shop until the chosen bay was reached. Engines without their tenders went in chimney first as most work was on the front ends. A capstan was used to drag the unpowered and un-braked engine into position. This was a delicate task as stopping a heavy slow moving un-braked mechanical horse could be somewhat problematic. A wooden scotch was used, with a risk that if not successful the engine could continue into and potentially through the Erecting Shop's far wall.

The Erecting Shop contained ten somewhat cramped locomotive bays and whilst tank and small tender engines could be accommodated completely within the building, larger tender engines would have the back end of their cabs protruding through the open doors. The space between each bay was limited and could restrict operations if two fitters were working with equipment on adjacent engines concurrently. The Erecting Shop roof was higher than the other shops to accommodate an overhead crane. Its activities were co-ordinated by a chargeman on each shift with a team of fitters and fitters' assistants.

The locomotive factory foreman's office, where the works clerk was also located, was an elevated structure within the adjacent Fitting Shop. It was accessed by a flight of open stairs and its windows faced towards the shop floor, giving a clear view of work activity below. The elevated office layout was a design feature found in many manufacturing and repair workshops at the time. A traditional externally mounted works hooter was sounded in the morning to summon staff to work, at lunchtime and at the close of work. It was said it had a deeper tone than that for the Heenan's factory nearby.

I am indebted to assistance from the ever knowledgeable Brian Penney and to Richard Parker who together recorded much of the Worcester's Shed and Works role and practices.

The Traverser gave access to the Erecting Shop and was electric powered. Locomotives were manoeuvred on to it from the works holding sidings, out of view to the right. The traverser was then moved across to the bay required for engine berthing. FRED COLE COLLECTION

No 6906 *Chicheley Hall* in the cramped almost filled to capacity Erecting Shop on 8 September 1963. No 6906 was a Banbury based engine, demonstrating locomotives outside the district were often dealt with here. The two wooden packing cases in the foreground are intriguingly stencilled, 'AEC Ltd. and ACW Sales Ltd, Southall, Middlesex, England' (misspelt South Hall on the second box). These would originally have been used to transport spares for the ex-GWR AEC diesel railcars withdrawn the year previously. MANCHESTER LOCOMOTIVE SOCIETY.

No 5042 *Winchester Castle* protrudes out of the Erecting Shop on 12 July 1964 giving a wonderful profile of the cab interior. It had just two weeks earlier been transferred from Hereford to Gloucester Horton Road, where it would continue working until its June 1965 withdrawal; the oldest 'Castle' and the last 5000 number series one to remain operational. HUGH BALLANTYNE. RAILPHOTOPRINTS

The Erecting Shop from a more elevated position on 12 July 1964, giving a good view of work being undertaken. Under repair are Westbury's No 5932 *Haydon Hall*, Hereford's 0-6-0PT No 3683 and Gloucester Horton Road's No 5042 *Winchester Castle*. The latter is undergoing a major mileage examination requiring all valves, pistons, connecting and coupling rods to be removed for refurbishing. Smaller parts associated with the attention to *Haydon Hall* lie on the locomotive's running plate. HUGH BALLANTYNE. RAILPHOTOPRINTS

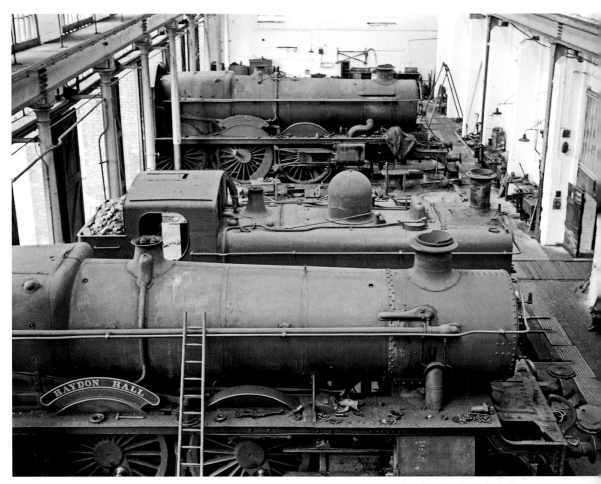

No 7007 *Great Western* positioned under the heavy lifting gear in front of the works building in 1959. A pair of driving wheels has been removed and the timbers supporting the rear underside of the cab and the chain securing the front end are indicative of the recent lifting operation. KEITH LANGSTON. RAILPHOTOPRINTS

No 5094 *Tretower Castle* of St Phillip's Marsh in a somewhat dramatic and precarious position as a pair of driving wheels is manoeuvred under the engine around 1960/61. Positioning the wheels are fitter's mate Ernie Payne and fitter Ron Ashby, whilst factory foreman Don Green in the light jacket looks on. Fitter Dick Giblett is stood on top of the hoist. Brian Penney happened to be in Don Green's office when he was having a desk clear out and this photo was heading for the bin until fortunately rescued. BRIAN PENNEY COLLECTION

No 6973 *Bricklehampton Hall* awaiting attention at Worcester Works on 27 March 1965. It had been transferred from Severn Tunnel Junction to Bristol Barrow Road during that week and was either scheduled for heavy maintenance or may have failed in traffic whilst working a freight train through the area. The hoist and erecting shop are in the background. R.N. PRITCHARD

No 7013 *Bristol Castle* under the locomotive hoist awaiting attention on 12 July 1964. It had been transferred from Old Oak Common to the LMR at Tyseley on 20 June to assist with Summer Saturday holiday train working to the South Coast but seems to have done little work. It would remain at the works until late August, but did then head the 7.05am Birmingham Snow Hill to Weymouth, via Swindon, on Saturday 29 August 1964. It would be withdrawn that September at the end of summer timetable operations. HUGH BALLAYTYNE. RAILPHOTOPRINTS

No 7023 *Penrice Castle,* home based at Worcester, receives attention on the works site in 1964. A fitter works on the pony truck whilst lifting chains hang down at the front of the engine. *Penrice Castle* would be transferred to Oxley in June 1964. RALPH WARD

No 7029 *Clun Castle* outside the works stripped down with inside cylinders removed on 19 September 1965. Gloucester Horton Road based and heading for preservation, it would spend much of the last few months of steam operations on special train working. R.N. PRITCHARD

Departmental Coach DW84 on the Worcester Works site in April 1964. Little gems like this were still to be found by the eagle eyed at the time. This early GWR Dean era five compartment, third class, four wheeled coach dated from 1900. It was converted to a tool and stores van in 1942 and is stencilled 'M&E', confirming it as a departmental vehicle in the Mechanical & Electrical Engineers department. It also carried the stencil 'New Works' at the far end. TIM FAREBROTHER

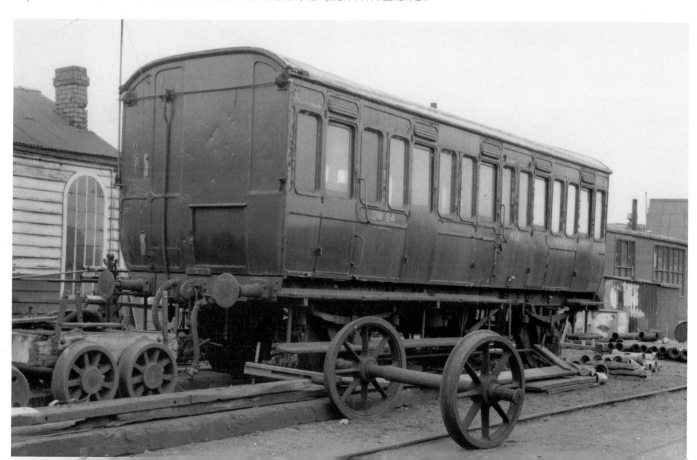

Worcester 'Castles' – The Cream of the Crop and the Paddington Expresses

No 7007 *Great Western* will shortly move away light engine to Ranelagh Bridge stabling point for turning and servicing on 1 July 1962, having recently terminated with the 8am Hereford to Paddington 'The Cathedrals Express'. The service was regarded as Worcester's premier turn for both locomotive and footplate crew. NIGEL KENDALL

Worcester 'Castles' – Locomotive Allocation
January 1960

4088 *Dartmouth Castle*	5071 *Spitfire*
4089 *Donnington Castle*	5081 *Lockheed Hudson*
5037 *Monmouth Castle*	7002 *Devizes Castle*
5039 *Rhuddlan Castle*	7005 *Sir Edward Elgar*
5042 *Winchester Castle*	7007 *Great Western*
	Total: 10

Worcester had a long association with Collett's 7P 'Castle' class 4-6-0s for its Hereford-Worcester-Paddington services. On 1 January 1948, the depot was home to six of these powerful express passenger engines. Alongside them were two of their predecessors, the now aging 1907 Churchward 'Star' class 4-6-0s. The depot's last 'Star', No 4007 *Swallowfield Park*, would be withdrawn in September 1951. The allocation stabilised at seven or eight 'Castles' through most of the 1950s, increasing to ten in November 1959. The January 1960 allocation is set out in full in the first table. This remained around ten with minor variations until mid-1963, reflecting the consistent two hourly Paddington train service frequency throughout the period. A slightly reduced eight 'Castles' allocation marked the start of the summer 1963 timetable. Type 3 'Hymek' D7000 diesel hydraulic training was now under way with a view to taking over the Paddington services and we will return to this transitional period later.

Whilst the allocation remained fairly consistent over the years, there was a regular turnover in individual engines. No less than twenty-six different 'Castles' passed through the depot's hands between January 1960 and their demise in October 1964. During a nine month period between January and September 1960 there was no less than a sixty per cent allocation turnover. Six were transferred away with Nos 4085 *Berkeley Castle*, 4089 *Donnington Castle*, 5037 *Monmouth Castle* and 5042 *Winchester Castle* going to

Old Oak Common, 5039 *Rhuddlan Castle* to Landore and 5081 *Lockheed Hudson* to Cardiff Canton. Departing locomotives Nos 4085 *Berkeley Castle*, 5037 *Monmouth Castle* and 5042 *Winchester Castle* were all high mileage Worcester engines and on leaving went via Swindon Works for Heavy General or Heavy Intermediate overhauls. Meanwhile six fresh 'Castles' replaced them; Nos 4085 *Berkeley Castle* from Gloucester Horton Road, which subsequently left again within the period, 7004 *Eastnor Castle*, 7013 *Bristol Castle* and 7027 *Thornbury Castle* from Old Oak Common and 7006 *Lydford Castle* and 7023 *Penrice Castle* from Cardiff Canton. Nos 7013 *Bristol Castle* and 7027 *Thornbury Castle* came in fine order via Swindon Works Heavy General overhauls. These changes resulted in a higher concentration of post-war built 7000 series 'Castles' at Worcester; something that would remain a feature for the remaining years. The high locomotive turnover within a limited period would have undoubtedly brought challenges for the depot's mechanical staff, losing familiar steeds and acquiring fresh ones with different mechanical and performance quirks that gave steam engines their uniqueness.

Through this period of change, Worcester's jealously guarded favourites, Nos 7005 *Sir Edward Elgar* and 7007 *Great Western*, remained secure. No 7005 had been a Worcester engine from new in June 1946 until its August 1964 paper transfer to Southall, followed by a September 1964 withdrawal. In practice, the engine never left Worcester and was stored withdrawn for several months. It entered service as

Lamphey Castle, becoming *Sir Edward Elgar* in August 1957 to mark the one hundredth anniversary of the Worcestershire composer's birth. The depot's other favourite, No 7007 *Great Western*, was the last express passenger engine to be built at Swindon Works under GWR ownership in July 1946; the final batch of 'Castles' Nos 7008 to 7037 being built under BR ownership between May 1948 and August 1950. No 7007 entered service as *Ogmore Castle*, being renamed *Great Western* on 1 January 1948, coincidental with the company losing its independent identity. No 7007 was initially allocated to Stafford Road and then Old Oak Common before moving to Worcester in February 1950, where it became a firm fixture until its February 1963 withdrawal.

Other well remembered Worcester 'Castles' during the 1960s included Nos 7002 *Devizes Castle* from November 1959 to March 1964, 7004 *Eastnor Castle* from July 1960 to September 1963, 7013 *Bristol Castle* from May 1960 to September 1963, 7023 *Penrice Castle* from August 1960 to June 1964 and 7027 *Thornbury Castle* from April 1960 to August 1963.

During this period, Worcester became one of the depots where Alfloc water treatment fitted 'Castles' were concentrated. This was another factor influencing the depot's allocation at the time. The Alfloc system required depot equipment to be installed and for both depot staff and firemen to be trained and familiar with the system. Alfloc was a boiler water treatment developed jointly by BR and ICI to reduce the build-up of scale in the boiler, tubes and inner boiler surfaces in hard water areas. Alfloc treated locomotives could be programmed for two weekly instead of the usual weekly boiler washouts, significantly increasing locomotive availability. The treatment was added in the form of briquettes placed in a long sieve hanging inside the tender water filling opening. The dissolved solution fed from the tender into the boiler using the

locomotive's injectors. It was necessary to regularly blow down the boiler to remove scale and other impurities that the chemicals had removed from surfaces. Alfloc fitted locomotives also received 'everlasting' blow down valves located above the foundation ring at the front of the firebox. Depots were required to test boiler water daily and the briquette dosage duly adjusted. The depot boiler smith was responsible for depot tasks and firemen undertook the necessary actions out on the road. The treatment could make the boiler prone to priming, causing boiler water to be lost through the safety valves, and firemen would in those circumstances release an anti-foam chemical agent from a 'tundish' on the cab front of the tender.

Whilst the allocation of around ten 'Castles' slightly fluctuated in numbers, their daily diagrammed workload remained consistent throughout the 1960s until dieselisation threatened. Rare examples of monthly footplate returns have survived for October and November 1960 and February 1962, each showing Worcester having a consistent six 'Castle' passenger locomotive turns. A complete set of monthly returns survives from January 1963 and this shows that right up to June 1963, the six passenger turns held good. It was only during the summer 1963 timetable, when 'Hymek' diesel hydraulic driver training and partial service introduction occurred, that the planned workload dropped marginally to five turns. In practice, however, during that summer, steam and 'Hymek' working became somewhat interchangeable dependent on training requirements and locomotive availability.

Returning to the pre-dieselisation period when the depot had six daily turns; we know that at least four of these were the depot's principal Worcester to Paddington turns. All Hereford to Paddington services in the forward direction changed engines at Worcester Shrub Hill. Typically, in the summer 1962 timetable, the 8am, 10.5am,

12.5pm and 2.5pm Hereford to Paddington, leaving Worcester Shrub Hill at 9.10am, 11.10am, 1.10pm and 3.10pm respectively, were all regular Worcester 'Castle' turns. The 8am Hereford to Paddington 'The Cathedrals Express' was the depot's prime London working for locomotive and crew. The first service of the day, the 6.20am Hereford to Paddington, rarely seems to have been recorded and may or may not have also been a Worcester 'Castle'. Indeed, Old Oak Common 'Castles' were known to overnight in the area and would have needed a back working during the morning.

Worcester's locomotive balances at the Paddington end varied between specific services and over the years. If the locomotive was on a short turnaround at Paddington, it was usual practice for the Worcester locomotive and crew to remain together for the round trip. Speaking to several former Worcester top link firemen, they recall that in most instances, when their engine was released from the stop blocks at Paddington, they would run tender first light engine the short distance to Ranelagh Bridge servicing point. There the engine would be turned, watered and prepared for their return working by a local crew whilst the Worcester men took their meal break. Alternatively, Worcester crews were sometimes relieved on arrival at Paddington, taking their break there whilst local ferrymen undertook the round trip to Ranelagh Bridge. The Worcester crew would then re-join their locomotive on its return. A third option, when less often the locomotive was diagrammed for a long layover in London, could see the engine work light engine to Old Oak Common for servicing. There were no coaling facilities at Ranelagh Bridge, but this was not a problem for a round trip from Worcester.

It is worth at this point clarifying how Paddington service portion joining and dividing worked at Worcester Shrub Hill, as this dictated locomotive working arrangements. Travelling towards Paddington, the three or four coach portion from Hereford would come to a stand at Shrub Hill's mid-platform signal on the long up platform. The engine from Hereford would then be released via the mid-platform crossover on to the centre through road. The main Worcester starting portion, which included the restaurant or buffet car, would have arrived empty stock at the leading end of the platform. The forward Worcester or Old Oak Common 'Castle' would already be at its head. This portion would then cautiously set back until it coupled up to the Hereford portion at the rear. A brake test would be undertaken and when satisfactorily completed, the train was ready to depart. All up Hereford to Paddington services therefore had to change engines at Worcester. Ten minutes was the standard station allowance for these movements. In the case of 'The Cathedrals Express' a Kidderminster portion was also conveyed.

In the reverse direction, life was somewhat simpler. Services from Paddington arrived at Shrub Hill with the Hereford portion leading and the Worcester portion rear. The train would be split on arrival and the Hereford portion continued forward. This enabled through engine working from Paddington to Hereford for both Old Oak Common and Worcester 'Castles' if required. This was diagrammed on around half the services, with the remainder worked forward by Hereford or Worcester 'Halls'; these often completing several round trips per day. Worcester would regularly substitute 'Granges' on its workings. The two hourly Paddington to Hereford services all had resource efficient one hour turnarounds at Hereford for both coaching stock and locomotives. It was the practice there for the incoming engine to take water on arrival and then depart light engine for turning via the Brecon Curve triangle or the turntable on the down side to the north of the station. Meanwhile the Hereford station pilot repositioned the stock for departure.

This meant Worcester 'Castle' diagrams often comprised a first leg from Worcester to Paddington, then Paddington back to Hereford and finally Hereford to Worcester. A through Old Oak Common 'Castle' might slightly differently work Paddington to Hereford, back as far as Worcester, then after the mandatory engine change there, take forward the next Worcester to Paddington journey leg two hours later. The 3.15pm, 5.15pm and 7.15pm from Paddington all terminated at Hereford after the last up Paddington service of the day had departed. Locomotive stabling arrangements for this awkward imbalance varied, but in most years, one of the three would return light engine to Worcester, whilst two, usually one Worcester and one Old Oak Common 'Castle', would stable overnight on Hereford shed. At the weekend, my regular Sunday Hereford shed visits often note a pair of Worcester or Old Oak Common 'Castles' in light steam awaiting back workings that day or possibly Monday morning.

Whilst Worcester 'Castles' were not usually diagrammed for menial duties, a spare or high mileage engine confined to restricted duties might sometimes cover a 'Hall' 5MT 4-6-0 turn on secondary passenger workings. The 5.40pm Hereford to Worcester local service was worked by No 7005 *Sir Edward Elgar* on 20 September 1963 and by No 7023 *Penrice Castle* on 7 April 1964. Meanwhile, on 23 April 1964, No 7023 *Penrice Castle* headed the 8am Evesham to Birmingham Snow Hill, via Stratford-upon-Avon, commuter train. It almost certainly returned with the evening balanced commuter working from Birmingham.

Following the transitional summer 1963 timetable, with Type 3 D7000 'Hymeks' increasingly dominating, it was planned that a fully dieselised Paddington service would apply from the start of the 1963/64 winter timetable.

On Saturday 7 September, the 10.5am Hereford to Paddington was planned as the last steam hauled service from Worcester amidst much fuss and press attendance. An immaculate No 7023 *Penrice Castle* was turned out in the hands of experienced Worcester driver Sid Haynes and fireman Brian Houseman. On arrival at Paddington, the engine went light to Old Oak Common, whilst the Worcester crew worked back the next Hymek hauled return service demonstrating the mixed traction duties for drivers at the time. *Penrice Castle* would return with the last down train of the day, the 7.15pm Paddington to Hereford.

The supposed all dieselised winter 1963/64 Paddington service started as planned rather fortuitously timed at an un-accelerated timetable schedule. Meanwhile, storm clouds were gathering amongst a poorly performing Western Region diesel hydraulic fleet. Fragile all-round diesel reliability was turning into a very specific issue with the Type 4 'Western' diesel hydraulic fleet. These were to have been the cornerstone of the winter 1963/64 accelerated Paddington to South Wales timetable. However, their availability was hovering around 50 per cent, mainly due to bogie suspension and final drive unit problems. Worse was to come when the whole fleet was stopped following the discovery of a worrying number of collapsed roller bearings in some hydraulic transmissions. The problem was soon contained to a smaller group of locomotives, but the damage had been done and officialdom's confidence in the front line diesel fleet wavered.

A decision was taken that the Hereford-Worcester-Paddington service would revert to steam haulage and the 'Hymeks' redeployed to bolster diesel shortfalls on other routes. Old Oak Common, Worcester and now Reading 'Castles' found themselves back in favour. Additionally, Hereford received four 'Castles', replacing an equivalent number of less powerful 'Hall' 4-6-0s. This was with a view to Hereford playing an enhanced role on Paddington services as well as benefitting their north and west route express workings. In the event, almost all Paddington services changed engines at Worcester in both directions. One of Hereford's 'Castles' and a Worcester 'Hall', often substituted as ever by a 'Grange', were each given an intensive diagram of up to three round trips daily between Hereford and Worcester. Each diagram had a tight resource-efficient hour's turnaround at each end on most journey legs. The new arrivals at Hereford in October and November 1963 were Nos 5000 *Launceston Castle*, 5054 *Earl of Ducie*, 5055 *Earl of Eldon* and 7022 *Hereford Castle*, the latter by coincidence now based at its named depot. Breaking the newly established change engine routine, the last down evening service, the 7.15pm Paddington to Hereford, was worked by an Old Oak Common 'Castle' through to Hereford, returning the next morning.

However, Worcester's extra steam duties were dealt with somewhat differently. Official documentation confirms that revised engine workings between there and Paddington were dealt with under short term planning arrangements. Surviving monthly permanent workload summaries for the depot surprisingly take no account of the increased steam locomotive workload. No additional 'Castles' were allocated to Worcester and rather strangely, its permanent allocation of seven in August was down to five by October 1963. During this period, Worcester's 'Modified Halls' were more frequently seen on Paddington services and several 'Castles' were periodically loaned from other depots. Certainly Gloucester Horton Road's Nos 7003 *Elmley Castle* and 7034 *Ince Castle* made a number

of appearances between Worcester and Paddington and for a while were regularly seen stabled on Worcester shed. At the London end, life was to say the least unpredictable. Reading's small allocation of 'Castles' began to appear regularly alongside Old Oak Common's. Additionally, 'Modified Halls' from Old Oak Common, Reading, Didcot and Oxford seemed to appear on a random basis dependent on what was available at the London end. Despite this somewhat unpredictable period, footplate crews were aware that the route had gained a special reputation as the last regularly steam hauled express passenger route into Paddington. Efforts were made to deliver acceptable performances despite the variable motive power provision.

Then, for a short while, the route took on a rather special profile as the Western Region, in co-operation with Ian Allan, made preparations for a 9 May 1964 high-speed 'Castle' special train from Paddington to Plymouth and back. This was to commemorate the 60th anniversary of *City of Truro's* famous high-speed run. Locomotive Inspectors assessed all surviving 'Castles' that had run under 40,000 miles since their last overhaul and a short list of eight was drawn up. This included no less than four Worcester engines: Nos 5054 *Earl of Ducie*, 7022 *Hereford Castle*, 7023 *Penrice Castle* and 7025 *Sudeley Castle*. Discrete test running was undertaken on service trains between Paddington and Worcester, with much locomotive preparation and servicing work undertaken at Worcester Works. It is known that lucky travellers experienced 100mph running descending Campden bank towards Honeybourne on at least one and probably more occasions. There is not space here to recount the special train on the day. However Worcester's No 5054 *Earl of Ducie* was entrusted with the final journey leg between Bristol and Paddington, via Badminton. It achieved

96mph between Hullavington and Little Somerford, but just failing on the day to reach that magical 100mph.

The 'Hymeks' never actually disappeared completely from Paddington services during that 1963/64 winter timetable crisis period and by April 1964 they were returning in increasing numbers, although steam haulage was still the norm on many services. The route would at last return to a planned all diesel-hauled service from the June 1964 summer timetable change. Nevertheless, occasional steam substitution for diesel failures would continue to occur. With the increasing return of diesel traction Worcester's Nos 7011 *Banbury Castle* and No 7023 *Penrice Castle* went into store in May 1964. However, the following month, they were both transferred across the LMR regional boundary to the ex-GWR Oxley shed. With them went a third Worcester 'Castle', No 5091 *Cleeve Abbey*, to Tyseley. In the same month, Hereford sent two of its now redundant 'Castles', Nos 5000 *Launceston Castle* and 5056 *Earl of Powis*, also to Oxley, whilst another two arrived there from Old Oak Common. This in a single month brought Oxley and Tyseley's combined 'Castle' allocation up from eight to fifteen engines. One might ask what the LMR was up to when 'Midlandisation' was usually the order of the day on their inherited ex-GWR routes. The answer lay in the LMR's realisation that their thinly-spread diesel resources could not cover their impending Summer Saturday holiday train workload. These would become the 'Castles' express passenger swansong. They would be diagrammed to cover all Summer Saturday holiday services from Wolverhampton Low Level to the West of England, via Stratford-upon-Avon, as far as Bristol. They also assisted with working similar holiday services from Wolverhampton Low Level and Birmingham Snow Hill to the South Coast as far as Oxford or Kensington

Olympia, dependent on final destination and route taken.

The final dieselisation of summer 1964 timetable Hereford to Paddington services was the final nail in the coffin of Worcester as an express passenger steam depot. By late June 1964, there were just four 'Castles' left: Nos 5054 *Earl of Ducie*, 7005 *Sir Edward Elgar*, 7022 *Hereford Castle* and 7025 *Sudeley Castle*. Between them, they had just one diagrammed daily turn described as for 'specials'. In theory, this was to cover any additional special train work that might come the depot's way, but in reality, its primary role was as locomotive standby for diesel failures on Paddington services. Now one of the largely surplus 'Castles' might be seen working one of the depot's seven long distance freight turns diagrammed for 'Halls' or 'Granges'. Clearly short of work, 7005 *Sir Edward Elgar* went on loan to Swindon for a while that summer and was noted heading the 8.45am Swindon to Weston-Super-Mare day-trip service on 10 August 1964. Worcester 'Castles' were also loaned out at weekends to assist the Western Region's London Division on their overstretched summer Saturday commitments working return South Coast to Wolverhampton Low Level, via Oxford or Kensington Olympia, holiday trains. Worcester 'Castles' recorded on these duties included No 7022 *Hereford Castle* on the 8.45am Margate to Wolverhampton Low Level on Saturday 20 June 1964, No 5054 *Earl of Ducie* on the 9.40am Eastbourne to Wolverhampton Low Level on Saturday 18 July 1964 and No 7005 *Sir Edward Elgar* the 8.45am Margate to Wolverhampton Low Level on Saturday 5 September 1964. On the same day, No 5054 *Earl of Ducie* worked the 9.28am Bournemouth to Manchester/Liverpool. How and when these Worcester engines managed to get back to their home depot is not recorded.

As the 1964 summer timetable drew to a close, the end was nigh for Worcester's 'Castles'. No 7005 *Sir Edward Elgar* was given a paper transfer to Southall on 29 August 1964, but withdrawn just over a week later on 7 September 1964. In practice, Worcester's favourite engine never left its home depot and was stored there until called away to that great scrapyard in the sky. Week ending 5 September 1964 also saw decisions taken on Worcester's three other remaining 'Castles'. No 7027 *Thornbury Castle* was withdrawn, whilst the two engines involved in the May high speed 'Castle' special train run, Nos 5054 *Earl of Ducie* and 7022 *Hereford Castle* the Swindon spare, were transferred to Gloucester Horton Road. That depot became a gathering ground for the final 'Castles' in service, although in reality there was little work and certainly nothing of quality

for them there. Despite the expenditure and hard work preparing *Earl of Ducie* for that special May high-speed run, it was unceremoniously withdrawn from its new depot just seven weeks after transfer on 24 October 1964. The reason for this rather odd premature withdrawal decision is not known. *Hereford Castle* survived at Gloucester on mostly secondary passenger and freight duties somewhat longer; being the last but one 'Castle' to be withdrawn in June 1965. This just left at Gloucester No 7029 *Clun Castle*. It alternated its time between special train working and Gloucester's secondary duties until its formal withdrawal into preservation on 31 December 1965; coincidental with the formal end of Western Region steam operations.

Worcester 'Castle' Class Locomotives Allocation

January 1961	January 1962
4088 *Dartmouth Castle* 7002 *Devizes Castle* 7004 *Eastnor Castle* 7005 *Sir Edward Elgar* 7006 *Lydford Castle* 7007 *Great Western* 7011 *Banbury Castle* 7013 *Bristol Castle* 7023 *Penrice Castle* 7027 *Thornbury Castle* Total: 10	7002 *Devizes Castle* 7004 *Eastnor Castle* 7005 *Sir Edward Elgar* 7006 *Lydford Castle* 7007 *Great Western* 7009 *Athelney Castle* 7011 *Banbury Castle* 7023 *Penrice Castle* 7027 *Thornbury Castle* Total: 9
February 1963	**January 1964**
7002 *Devizes Castle* 7004 *Eastnor Castle* 7005 *Sir Edward Elgar* 7013 *Bristol Castle* 7023 *Penrice Castle* 7025 *Sudeley Castle* 7027 *Thornbury Castle* 7031 *Cromwell's Castle* Total: 8	7002 *Devizes Castle* 7005 *Sir Edward Elgar* 7011 *Banbury Castle* 7023 *Penrice Castle* 7025 *Sudeley Castle* Total: 5
August 1964	**September 1964**
5054 *Earl of Ducie* 7005 *Sir Edward Elgar* 7022 *Hereford Castle* 7025 *Sudeley Castle* Total: 4	5054 to Gloucester Horton Road 5.9.64 7005 to Southall 29.8.64 & w'drawn 7.9.64 7022 to Gloucester Horton Road 5.9.64 7025 Withdrawn 5.9.64 Total: Nil

Worcester 'Castle' Class Locomotives
Allocated between 1960 – 1964
Pre-1960 arrival dates shown for those already allocated January 1960

4085 *Berkeley Castle* February 1960–August 1960 (to Old Oak Common)
4088 *Dartmouth Castle* March 1958–February 1961 (to Swindon)
4089 *Donnington Castle* December 1958–July 1960 (to Old Oak Common)
5037 *Monmouth Castle* June 1954–May 1960 (to Old Oak Common)
5039 *Rhuddlan Castle* December 1959–February 1960 (to Landore)
5042 *Winchester Castle* February 1959–April 1960 (to Old Oak Common)
5054 *Earl of Ducie* April 1964–September 1964 (to Gloucester Horton Road)
5071 *Spitfire* September 1959–December 1960 (to Gloucester Horton Road)
5081 *Lockheed Hudson* December 1954–August 1960 (to Cardiff Canton)
5091 *Cleeve Abbey* April 1964–June 1964 (to Tyseley)
5096 *Bridgwater Castle* April 1964–June 1964 (Withdrawn)
5099 *Compton Castle* February 1962–October 1962 (to Gloucester Horton Road)
7000 *Viscount Portal* February 1963–December 1963 (Withdrawn)
7002 *Devizes Castle* November 1959–March 1964 (Withdrawn)
7004 *Eastnor Castle* July 1960–September 1963 (to Reading)
7005 *Sir Edward Elgar* June 1946 Newly built–August 1964 (to Southall)*
7006 *Lydford Castle* July 1960–March 1962 (to Old Oak Common)
7007 *Great Western* February 1950–February 1963 (Withdrawn)
7009 *Athelney Castle* February 1962–November 1962 (to Gloucester Horton Road)
7011 *Banbury Castle* Dec. 1960–Oct. 1962 & Jan. 1964–June 1964 (to Oxley)
7013 *Bristol Castle* May 1960–September 1963 (to Old Oak Common)
7022 *Hereford Castle* April 1964–October 1964 (to Gloucester Horton Road)
7023 *Penrice Castle* August 1960–June 1964 (to Oxley)
7025 *Sudeley Castle* October 1962–September 1964 (Withdrawn)
7027 *Thornbury Castle* April 1960–August 1963 (to Reading)
7031 *Cromwell's Castle* March 1962–July 1963 (Withdrawn)
*7005 Named *Lamphey Castle* until August 1957 when renamed *Sir Edward Elgar*. Withdrawn officially from Southall September 1964, but thought to be a paper transfer only as stored Worcester after withdrawal.
Source: BR Records – Locomotive Record Cards

'The Cathedrals Express' Hereford – Worcester Shrub Hill – Paddington
Recorded Locomotive Sightings 1960 to 1965.
Note that all Services change engines at Worcester Shrub Hill
Conveys portions from Hereford and Kidderminster

7004 85A 7.45am Hfd–Padd 'Cathedrals Express', from Worcs. 9.7.60
7023 85A 7.45am Hereford–Paddington 'Cathedrals Express', Paddington 27.5.61
7011 85A 7.45am Hereford–Paddington 'Cathedrals Express', Oxford 6.61
7011 85A 7.45am Hereford–Paddington 'Cathedrals Express', Cholsey 22.6.61
5001 81A 7.45am Hereford–Paddington 'Cathedrals Express', arrive Worcester SH 17.8.61
7011 85A 8am Hereford–Paddington 'Cathedrals Express', Paddington 26.9.61
7007 85A 8am Hereford–Paddington 'Cathedrals Express', Campden Bank 1962
7023 85A 8am Hereford–Paddington 'Cathedrals Express', West Ealing 24.2.62
7031 85A 8am Hereford–Paddington 'Cathedrals Express', arrive Worcester SH 25.2.62
7027 85A 8am Hereford–Paddington 'Cathedrals Express', Didcot 27.3.62
7007 85A 8am Hereford–Paddington 'Cathedrals Express', West Ealing 9.5.62
7013 85A 8am Hereford–Paddington 'Cathedrals Express', Campden 19.5.62
7031 85A 8am Hereford–Paddington 'Cathedrals Express', arrive Worcester SH 25.5.62
7011 85A 8am Hereford–Paddington 'Cathedrals Express', arrive Worcester SH 8.6.62
7013 85A 8am Hereford–Paddington 'Cathedrals Express', Paddington 16.6.62
7013 85A 8am Hereford–Paddington 'Cathedrals Express', Southall 30.6.62
7007 85A 8am Hereford–Paddington 'Cathedrals Express', Paddington 1.7.62
7009 85A 8am Hereford–Paddington 'Cathedrals Express', arr. Worcester SH Sum.1962
7034 85B 8am Hereford–Paddington 'Cathedrals Express', Paddington 6.4.63
7013 85A 8am Hereford–Paddington 'Cathedrals Express', Moreton-in-Marsh 13.4.63
6992 85A 8am Hereford–Paddington 'Cathedrals Express', arrive Worcester SH 30.4.63
7005 85A 8am Hereford–Paddington 'Cathedrals Express', Reading 4.5.63
7002 85A 8am Hereford–Paddington 'Cathedrals Express', to Worcester 9.5.63
7025 85A 8am Hereford–Paddington 'Cathedrals Express', Oxford 5.63
7005 85A 8am Hereford–Paddington 'Cathedrals Express', from Worcester SH 7.9.63
7005 85A 8am Hereford–Paddington 'Cathedrals Express', Paddington 28.9.63
7025 85A 8am Hereford–Paddington 'Cathedrals Express', Paddington 1.10.63
7005 85A 8am Hereford–Paddington 'Cathedrals Express', Paddington 2.10.63
7005 85A 8am Hereford–Paddington 'Cathedrals Express', Paddington 19.10.63
7000 85A 8am Hereford–Paddington 'Cathedrals Express', Paddington 26.10.63
7025 85A 8am Hereford–Paddington 'Cathedrals Express', Paddington 29.10.63
7004 81D 8am Hereford–Paddington 'Cathedrals Express', Paddington 30.10.63
5933 81F 8am Hereford–Paddington 'Cathedrals Express', Paddington 31.10.63
7920 85A 8am Hereford–Paddington 'Cathedrals Express', Paddington 1.11.63
7023 85A 8am Hereford–Paddington 'Cathedrals Express', arr. Worcester SH 22.2.64
7003 85B 8am Hereford–Paddington 'Cathedrals Express', arr. Worcester SH 29.2.64
7920 85A 8am Hereford–Paddington 'Cathedrals Express', Paddington 11.4.64
7023 85A 8am Hereford–Paddington 'Cathedrals Express', Paddington 20.4.64
80102 6D 8am Hereford–Paddington 'Cathedrals Express', arr. Worcester SH 9.1.65

No 5054 *Earl of Ducie* starts our photographic review of Worcester-allocated 'Castles'. It entered traffic in June 1936, having a relatively short but high profile time at Worcester from April to September 1964. The first few months were spent being prepared and running in for the 9 May 1964 Plymouth to Paddington High Speed 'Castle' special. It then became the first choice engine for enthusiast charter train workings over subsequent months. It left Worcester in September 1964 for Gloucester Horton Road where it was very quickly and unceremoniously withdrawn in October 1964. STEVE BARTLETT COLLECTION

No 5081 *Lockheed Hudson*, released to traffic in May 1939, was based at Worcester from December 1954 to August 1960. It then moved to Cardiff Canton and later Cardiff East Dock before November 1963 withdrawal. Seen here outside Swindon Works on 25 October 1959, having just received a Heavy General overhaul, it would be formally released back to Worcester two weeks later. MANCHESTER LOCOMOTIVE SOCIETY

No 5091 *Cleeve Abbey.* A December 1938 build, it had a brief but useful spell at Worcester from April to June 1964, where it is seen just after transfer from Cardiff East Dock. It would prove its worth working Paddington services covering diesel shortfalls. Moving on to Tyseley in June 1964, it spent that summer working holiday trains from the West Midlands to the South Coast before October 1964 withdrawal. TIM FAREBROTHER

No 5096 *Bridgwater Castle* was another short term April to June 1964 Worcester resident. Also arriving from Cardiff East Dock it would be withdrawn from Worcester in June 1964, its duties done. Seen here ready to depart Worcester Shrub Hill with the 10.05am Hereford to Paddington on 29 April 1964, it played its part in keeping the Paddington services operational during the difficult diesel shortfall period. R.G. NELSON. TERRY WALSH

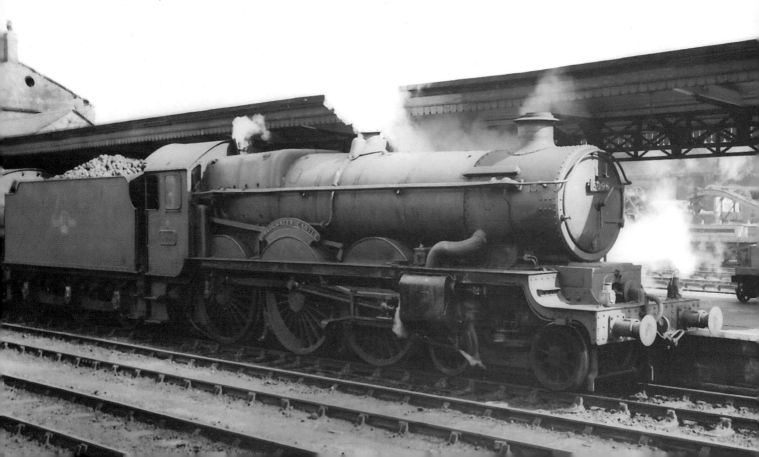

No 7000 *Viscount Portal* was one of an increasing number of newer 7000 series 'Castles' that would dominate the Worcester allocation. Built in May 1946, it was a Worcester engine from March 1963 to its December 1963 withdrawal. It is seen here at Worcester Shrub Hill on the 10.05am Hereford to Paddington on 13 November 1963. R.G. NELSON. TERRY WALSH

No 7002 *Devizes Castle* at Worcester on 17 May 1964. Despite still carrying number and name plates it had been withdrawn two months earlier on 10 March 1964. A June 1946 build, it spent many years in South Wales at Landore and Carmarthen until November 1959 transfer to Worcester. Here it became a familiar engine on Paddington services until its March 1964 withdrawal. ROY PALMER

No 7004 *Eastnor Castle* was another June 1946 build, spending from July 1960 to September 1963 at Worcester and another regular on Paddington services. It is seen here in March 1963 on Worcester shed with plenty of surplus steam in evidence. RAILPHOTOPRINTS

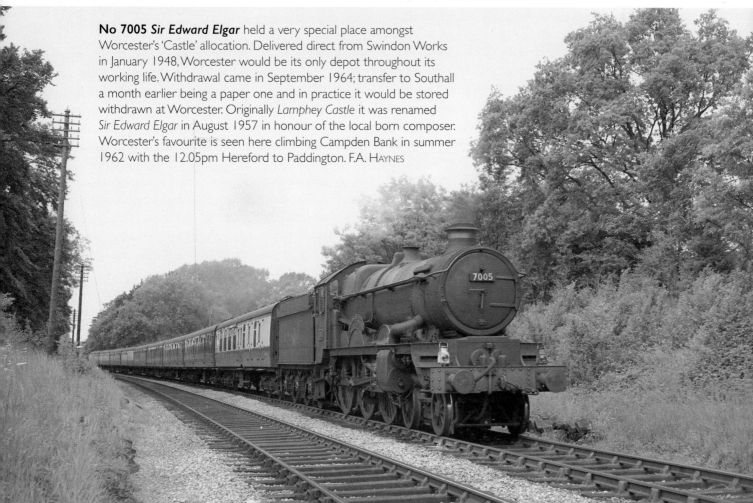

No 7005 *Sir Edward Elgar* held a very special place amongst Worcester's 'Castle' allocation. Delivered direct from Swindon Works in January 1948, Worcester would be its only depot throughout its working life. Withdrawal came in September 1964; transfer to Southall a month earlier being a paper one and in practice it would be stored withdrawn at Worcester. Originally *Lamphey Castle* it was renamed *Sir Edward Elgar* in August 1957 in honour of the local born composer. Worcester's favourite is seen here climbing Campden Bank in summer 1962 with the 12.05pm Hereford to Paddington. F.A. HAYNES

Farewell Old Friend. Worcester fitter Frank Waters removing *Sir Edward Elgar's* number and name plates on 17 November 1964, two months after withdrawal. Frank was a real shed character who in every picture he features is armed with his ever present pipe. FRED COLE COLLECTION

No 7006 *Lydford Castle* was yet another of the 7000 series 'Castles' that made Worcester its home. Released to traffic in June 1946, it arrived at Worcester in June 1960 from Cardiff Canton. It would move on to Old Oak Common in March 1962. Seen here on shed at Worcester on 26 June 1960, within days of its inwards transfer, it is chalked up on the cab side for a boiler washout. The depot's unusual Stothert & Pitt coaling hoist is in the background. MANCHESTER LOCOMOTIVE SOCIETY

No 7007 *Great Western* was another rather special 'Castle' based at Worcester from February 1950 until its February 1963 withdrawal. It was the last express passenger engine to be built at Swindon Works under GWR ownership in July 1946; the final batch of 'Castles' Nos 7008 to 7037 being built as BR locomotives between May 1948 and August 1950. Entering service as *Ogmore Castle*, it was renamed *Great Western* on 1 January 1948, the day the company finally lost its independent identity. It is seen here on Oxford shed around 1956. MANCHESTER LOCOMOTIVE SOCIETY

No 7007 *Great Western* was an exceptionally rare visitor to Caerphilly Works for a Light Casual overhaul from 28 February to 27 March 1962. The works usually handled South Wales based tank engines and the reason this Worcester 'Castle' found its way here is not known. Behind it is 1897 built ex-Taff Vale Railway 0-6-2T No 28 (GWR No 450). It had been withdrawn and sold into private ownership by the GWR in 1926, finally being withdrawn by the National Coal Board in 1960. Accepted into the National Locomotive Collection it was currently awaiting restoration. R.W.A. Jones. ONLINE TRANSPORT ARCHIVE

No 7011 *Banbury Castle* 'released to traffic in June 1948'; was allocated to Worcester from December 1960 to September 1962, when it was prematurely withdrawn whilst in Swindon Works for a Heavy General overhaul. Reinstated two weeks later, it moved on to Reading before returning to Worcester in January 1964 before a final June 1964 move to Oxley. There it was re-invigorated, working Summer Saturday holiday trains from Wolverhampton to the West of England and South Coast. This was followed by express freight and parcels work until final withdrawal from Oxley in February 1965. It is seen here on shed at Worcester on 3 May 1964. RALPH WARD

No **7013** *Bristol Castle* was yet another Worcester 'Castle' with a story to tell. Recorded as entering service in July 1946, it had whilst in Swindon Works in February 1952 changed identities with April 1924 built No 4082 *Windsor Castle* in preparation to work King George VI's funeral train. The identities were not changed back and the re-titled No 7013 *Bristol Castle* would be based at Worcester from February 1952 to October 1957 and again from May 1960 to September 1963. It was then re-allocated to Old Oak Common, having been put in store at Worcester the previous month. It would ultimately be withdrawn from Gloucester in September 1964. It is pictured here in pristine condition working the 'Cathedrals Express'. MANCHESTER LOCOMOTIVE SOCIETY

No **7022** *Hereford Castle*, released to traffic in June 1949, arrived at Worcester from Hereford in April 1964; another of the engines with No 5054 short listed for the 9 May 1964 High Speed Castle special train. *Hereford Castle* would be the unused standby engine at Swindon. Seen here on shed at Worcester on 4 July 1964, complete with replacement wooden smokebox number plate and tarnished white buffers from the special train commitment, it would be transferred to Gloucester in October 1964, where it performed some useful secondary work until June 1965 withdrawal. NORMAN PREEDY. RAILPHOTOPRINTS

No 7023 *Penrice Castle* being prepared at Worcester to take the 7.45am Hereford to Paddington, the 'Cathedrals Express', forward from Worcester Shrub Hill on 12 October 1960. In the background is Worcester's No 6984 *Owsden Hall*. *Penrice Castle* entered traffic in June 1949 and was Worcester based from August 1960 until June 1964 transfer to Oxley. It was yet another export to the LMR's ex-GWR Oxley shed for working that summer's holiday expresses from Wolverhampton Low Level to the West of England and the South Coast. It would be withdrawn from Oxley in February 1965. RON HERBERT

No 7025 *Sudeley Castle* started its operational life in August 1949 and was a regular at Worcester on Paddington services between October 1962 and September 1964 withdrawal. It is seen here on shed at Worcester in April 1964. RALPH WARD

No 5054 *Earl of Ducie* magnificently captured at Great Somerford with the 9 May 1964 High Speed Special train from Plymouth to Paddington. The Worcester engine took over the reins for the final non-stop leg from Bristol Temple Meads to Paddington, via Badminton, achieving a top speed of 96mph. HUGH BALLANTYNE. RAILPHOTOPRINTS

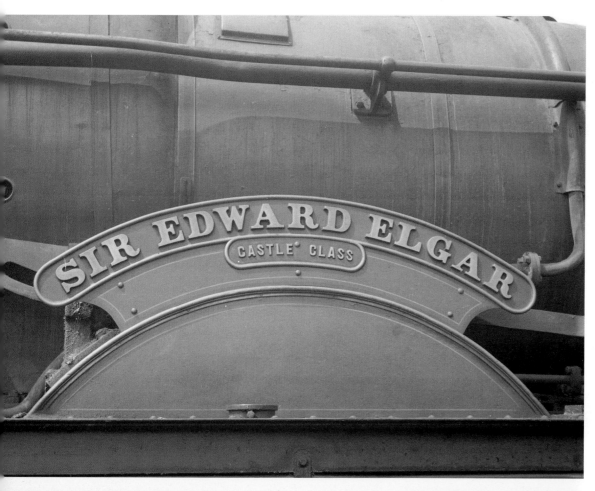

Sir Edward Elgar's nameplate carried by that much loved Worcester engine, photographed whilst on shed there in 1964. A Worcester based locomotive throughout its working life; No 7005 *Sir Edward Elgar* was renamed from *Lamphey Castle* in recognition of the locally born composer in August 1957. RALPH WARD

Great Western's magnificent nameplate showing off to perfection the brass and paint work and the crest carried on the splasher. Photographed on 26 August 1956, No 7007 *Great Western* was a long term Worcester based engine from February 1950 until its February 1963 withdrawal. HAROLD BOWTELL. MANCHESTER LOCOMOTIVE SOCIETY

Hereford-Worcester-Paddington Services

Having looked more closely at a selection of individual Worcester 'Castles' we will now view them out on the road between Worcester and Paddington, working the two hourly express passenger services that they dominated. The photographs are displayed sequentially along the route from Worcester Shrub Hill through to Paddington, followed by a further selection on the return journey. Most are worked by Worcester engines but those from Old Oak Common and Reading, plus the odd interloper from a foreign depot, are also featured.

Worcester Shrub Hill. Home based No 7025 *Sudeley Castle* prepares to depart with a nine coaches Paddington Express on 1 June 1963. The train engine would have come on with the Worcester restaurant car portion at the leading end of the platform, then set back on to the three or four coach portion from Hereford on its arrival. The latter's engine would first have been released through the mid-platform crossover. A brake test of the complete train when coupled would be carried out before whistles blew and the train departed. Ten minutes station time was allowed at Shrub Hill for this somewhat involved move. R.C. RILEY. TRANSPORT TREASURY

On the Way. The same train pulls away from Worcester Shrub Hill for Paddington on 1 June 1963. The level and straight road ahead enables the Worcester crew to make a spirited start towards Norton Junction and the Cotswolds line. R.C. RILEY. TRANSPORT TREASURY

Norton Junction is passed at speed on a left hand curve by Worcester's No 7023 *Penrice Castle* with the 10.05am Hereford to Paddington in 1962. The engine has been steadily accelerating over the three miles since leaving Shrub Hill. The short link line down to Abbots Wood Junction and the Midland Railway route from Birmingham New Street to Bristol leaves the main route on the left. F.A. HAYNES

Stoulton 'between Worcester and Evesham' is passed at speed by Worcester's No 7004 *Eastnor Castle* with a Hereford to Paddington express in the 1960s. F.A. Haynes

Approaching Evesham with safety valves lifted is Worcester's immaculate No 7027 *Thornbury Castle* with the 10.05am Hereford to Paddington in late spring 1961. Evesham's single road engine shed can be seen in the background, whilst the former Midland Railway line from Ashchurch to Birmingham New Street via Redditch curves in on the left. F.A. Haynes

Evesham.
Worcester's No 7013 *Bristol Castle* in sparkling external condition drifts into the station with the 12.05pm Hereford to Paddington in spring 1962. The platform advertising hoardings are a nostalgic reminder of times past. F.A. HAYNES

Evesham. Worcester's rather grimy 'Castle' No 7005 *Sir Edward Elgar* decelerates into the station with a Hereford to Paddington express on 1 June 1963. The fireman appears to be shouting a message to a hidden station staff member. It was nearly a year since the engine's last Heavy Intermediate overhaul at Swindon Works and it would receive no further main works attention up to its September 1964 withdrawal. DAVE WALDREN

Campden Bank. Worcester's No 4088 *Dartmouth Castle* makes a vigorous ascent of the bank with a Hereford to Paddington express in 1960. The service's next station call would be Moreton-in-Marsh. The engine was Worcester based from March 1958 to February 1961, receiving a Heavy General overhaul at Swindon Works in August 1959. F.A. HAYNES

Campden Bank. You can almost hear the loud exhaust beat as Worcester's immaculate No 7002 *Devizes Castle* makes a powerful climb of Campden Bank with a Hereford to Paddington express in 1963. It was a Worcester engine from November 1959 until its March 1964 withdrawal and was clearly being kept in fine external condition by the depot. F.A. HAYNES

Chipping Campden Tunnel. A stranger in the camp as Wolverhampton Stafford Road 'Castle' No 5063 *Earl Baldwin* bursts out of Chipping Campden tunnel with the 2.05pm Hereford to Paddington on 4 May 1963. The next station call would be Moreton-in-Marsh. This service was booked for Worcester 'Castle' haulage and clearly a change of plan had been necessary on this occasion. GERALD T. ROBINSON

Approaching Oxford having previously called at Kingham is Worcester 'Castle' No 7005 *Sir Edward Elgar* with the 12.05pm Hereford to Paddington on 11 May 1963. GERALD T. ROBINSON

Oxford Station with two Hereford to Paddington services crossing on 2 June 1962, each worked by exceptionally clean Worcester 'Castles'. It was during the previous year that both received main works attention, their present turnout being down to Worcester's cleaning staff attention. On the right, undertaking station duties, is No 7031 *Cromwell's Castle* with the 10.05am Hereford to Paddington, whilst on the left No 5099 *Compton Castle* runs in with the 11.15am Paddington to Hereford. GERALD T. ROBINSON

Taplow between Maidenhead and Slough, with Worcester's No 7027 *Thornbury Castle* hurrying through at speed with a Hereford to Paddington express on 3 June 1962. Paddington would be the next stop and the end of the journey. NIGEL KENDALL

Paddington Station late at night on 14 April 1964 as Reading's No 5039 *Rhuddlan Castle* sits, having earlier terminated with the 6.05pm from Hereford due to arrive at 10pm. This was during the winter 1963/64 steam replacement timetable and soon such scenes would be no more. GERALD T. ROBINSON

Paddington Station. It's time to make our way back from Paddington towards Worcester. In another evocative late night scene Old Oak Common's No 7035 *Ogmore Castle* prepares to depart with the 7.15pm to Worcester and Hereford on Saturday 16 November 1963. The engine would work through to Hereford arriving there at 11.05pm. By complete coincidence, I made a Hereford shed visit the next day, Sunday, when *Ogmore Castle* was recorded as one of five 'Castles' seen in light steam there that day. DAVID NICHOLAS

Oxford with Old Oak Common's immaculate No 7008 *Swansea Castle* waiting to depart with a Paddington to Hereford express in June 1963. The fireman waits patiently, although somewhat distracted, for the right away from the station staff. Kingham will be the next station stop. GORDON EDGAR COLLECTION. RAILPHOTOPRINTS

Leaving Oxford is Worcester's No 7928 *Wolf Hall* with the 3.15pm Paddington to Hereford on 11 May 1963. This was a Worcester 'Castle' turn but the depot's 5MT 'Modified Hall' 4-6-0s were regarded as more than capable of handling these services when called upon to do so. GERALD T. ROBINSON

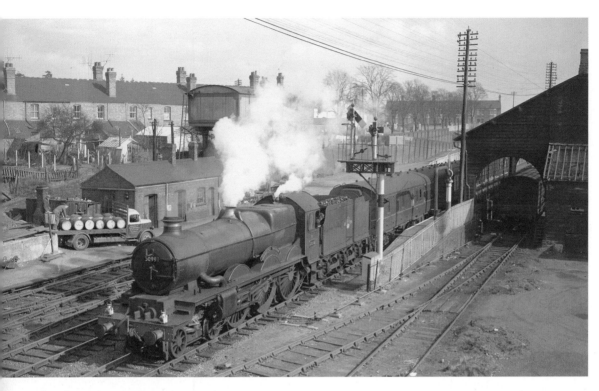

Evesham.
Worcester's No 5099 *Compton Castle* with ample steam to spare prepares to depart for Worcester with a Paddington to Hereford service in 1962. The lorry in the background bears the ownership 'Wholesale Fruit Merchants Evesham' and wooden barrels are in the process of being manhandled. F.A. HAYNES

Stoulton 'between Evesham and Worcester' is hurried through by Worcester's No 7011 *Banbury Castle* with a Paddington to Hereford express in 1961. Three miles ahead lay Norton Junction and then the final run into Worcester Shrub Hill. The chalked train head code 1A22 is misleadingly left over from the locomotive's previous journey leg from Worcester to Paddington, a common deficiency on these services. F.A. HAYNES

Norton Halt is passed by Worcester's No 7009 *Athelney Castle* with the 1.15pm Paddington to Hereford in spring 1962. Ahead lies the three miles easy run into Worcester Shrub Hill. There the footplate crew would change but the Worcester 'Castle' would work through to Hereford. There, after a short one hour's turnaround, it would bring back the 6.05pm Hereford to Paddington as far as Worcester Shrub Hill. This would complete its day's work which had started with a Worcester to Paddington journey leg that morning. F.A. HAYNES

Great Western Diesel Railcars

Diesel Railcars at rest in their servicing shed at the northern end of the Worcester Works site in October 1958. A third car can just be seen behind the left hand railcar and a fourth is likely to be behind the right hand car. All six on the allocation at this time returned to Worcester nightly and any excess vehicles were stabled on the sidings outside the shed. Servicing pits are evident on both shed roads. MANCHESTER LOCOMOTIVE SOCIETY

Ex-GWR Diesel Railcars – Worcester
Allocation – April 1960

W20W	W23W	W29W
W22W	W26W	W32W
		Total: 6

Whilst the main focus in this volume is on steam operations, there has to be a place for the once-familiar ex-GWR diesel railcars. In Great Western days, the sleek early railcars were affectionately known as 'Flying Bananas'. These attractive vehicles were a consistent presence on local passenger services in the Worcester area for many years; the depot's first railcar No7 arriving newly built in July 1935. The allocation settled down to around six cars throughout the 1950s and into the 1960s. Worcester would become their final operational base; the last six cars being withdrawn from service in October 1962.

Hardy Rail Motors, a subsidiary of AEC Southall, had been responsible for developing the railcar project in the early 1930s. They saw that diesel engines already used in heavy commercial vehicles, in particular AEC's London buses, could be capable of efficiently powering a lightweight single railcar. Extensive research was undertaken in co-operation with the Great Western Railway to develop a design of suitable lightweight and aerodynamic construction that would also be capable of meeting the rigours and safety requirements of an operational railway. Final public service trials took place in December 1933 and railcar No1 was officially released to traffic in February 1934 allocated to Southall shed, close to AEC's home base. There would be design variations between specific vehicles and builds over a number of years. Several were more comfortably equipped, including a buffet serving light refreshments, to launch a limited

stop businessmen's service between Birmingham Snow Hill and Cardiff. However the majority were intended for and would operate as single cars on branch and local passenger services and would become widely dispersed around the GWR system. Those wishing to delve further into the detailed design and development of these fascinating early diesel vehicles are directed to Colin Judge's definitive work *The History of Great Western AEC Diesel Railcars*.

A railcar servicing depot was soon established at Worcester in the Carriage & Wagon works. This was north of Shrub Hill station on the opposite side of the main line to the steam shed. It was already in use as a wagon repair workshop and now shared the building with the diesel railcars. The nearest shed road to the main line was designated for railcar servicing and maintenance, although in practice the nearest two shed roads were often occupied. Vehicle fuelling points were provided both inside and outside the shed with pits for underfloor maintenance within the depot. Stabling also took place on outside sidings.

Given the specialist nature of diesel engine maintenance at that time, this was carried out under the supervision of an AEC Southall Service Engineer. George Norris was the AEC representative that looked after the Worcester cars. He was out-based at Tyseley and was responsible for railcars operating from there, Leamington, Stourbridge, Cheltenham and Worcester. In 1958, all maintenance responsibilities were taken over by BR Western Region. George Norris stayed on, now becoming a direct British Railways employee continuing in the same role retitled District Diesel Mechanical Inspector. The work he oversaw at Worcester was carried out by a fitter and his mate on day and night shifts. These were part of a four week multi-skilled fitters' roster involving week one working at the diesel shed on days, week two steam shed nights, week three steam shed days and week four diesel shed nights. When a small allocation of newly built diesel shunting engines arrived at Worcester in 1960, they were also fuelled and serviced in the wagon shops area. Later in 1966, when the steam depot had closed, the former passenger shed was converted to a diesel servicing point.

During the 1950s, there were four daily diagrammed duties for the six railcars based at Worcester. These had reduced to three diagrams by the early 1960s. The railcars operated local services from Worcester to Malvern and Ledbury on the Hereford line, to Honeybourne, Evesham and Moreton-in-Marsh on the Cotswolds route, northwards towards Hartlebury, Droitwich and Kidderminster and also on the Bromyard branch. Local services on all these routes ran to an irregular timetable pattern timed to meet specific passenger flows. None of these local services was worked exclusively by diesel railcars, operations being shared with locomotive hauled local services. The latter were generally worked by 2-6-2 prairie or 0-6-0 pannier tanks. One does wonder if greater efficiencies could have been achieved by creating dedicated railcar routes in the area.

Many will be familiar with or have seen photographs of ex-GWR diesel railcars operating on the Severn Valley lines from Kidderminster and Bewdley. Most of these railcar trips did not penetrate beyond Bridgnorth on the Severn Valley's main route, although there was one daily trip to Shrewsbury. The railcars were also regular performers on the Severn Valley branches from Bewdley to Hartlebury and Bewdley to Tenbury Wells/Woofferton. Casual

observers might have assumed the railcar workings were Kidderminster based, but in fact it was Worcester allocated diesel railcars that worked these services. They travelled out each morning empty stock or on early scheduled services and returned to Worcester each evening for stabling. There were some steam locomotive-hauled Severn Valley services and these were resourced from Kidderminster with occasional through Shrewsbury workings. There were several diesel railcars based at Stourbridge, to the north of Kidderminster, but these worked exclusively towards Birmingham in the Old Hill and Dudley areas. In fact, in 1950, which is the only complete set of railcar workings that can be traced, no less than two and a half of the four daily Worcester railcar diagrams spent their time working the Severn Valley and its branches services. Turning to railcar trained footplate staff, there was a dedicated link of railcar drivers based at Worcester. In addition to the more obvious Worcester area railcar duties they also worked over all the Severn Valley routes with their vehicles.

The 1950 railcar diagrams reveal that at that time and for some years afterwards, one of the railcars started the day with a very much 'off piste' forty-eight miles empty stock movement to start its day's work. This left Worcester at 5.35am empty stock to Shelwick Junction, on the approach to Hereford, where it reversed and then ran up the North and West route to Ludlow arriving at 7.01am. There it formed the 7.25am Ludlow-Woofferton (reverse)-Kidderminster passenger service, remaining on Severn Valley duties all day. This bizarre early morning empty stock movement disappeared at some stage during the 1950s. Equally unusually, one railcar diagram originally finished with a 7.26pm passenger service from Woofferton to Worcester, via Leominster and Bromyard. The section from Leominster to Bromyard was over a scenic but little used section of the

Leominster to Worcester via Bromyard branch. This section would see an early withdrawal of passenger services in September 1952. On routes leading to the Severn Valley, passenger services were withdrawn between Woofferton and Tenbury Wells in July 1961 and beyond there to Bewdley in August 1962. These service withdrawals just fell within the tail end of the railcar era that would see all remaining vehicles at Worcester withdrawn in October 1962.

These were nevertheless the only actual service withdrawals within the Worcester railcars' sphere of influence that could have been said to contribute to their demise. Elsewhere, and specifically on the local services around Worcester, it would be the arrival of new generation BR single car and diesel multiple units that directly lead to their withdrawal. Ironically, a number of steam hauled local passenger services that had worked alongside the railcars, including some on the Bromyard branch, would remain steam operated some years longer.

The ex-GWR railcars were undoubtedly ahead of their time when introduced in stages between 1934 and 1942 and ultimately numbered thirty-eight vehicles. They led the way to cleaner and more efficient service operations with significantly reduced fuel and staffing costs. The most obvious economy was greater crewing efficiency, with services now only requiring a driver and a guard. The question might be asked why more than the comparatively small fleet of thirty-eight vehicles were not introduced by the GWR at a faster rate. Clearly, the company had initially adopted a sensibly cautious policy of phased introduction until the innovative design and type of propulsion involved had proven itself. It was unfortunate that with the final railcar being introduced in 1942 other Second World War priorities took over. Then, as the railways were slowly recovering from war shortages, it would be rail nationalisation that came along with the focus turned to a system-wide solution from which the new generation of diesel multiple units emerged. These ex-GWR diesel railcars will be fondly remembered by those who travelled on them and well respected by railwaymen who worked with them in service operation. They have to be recognised as one of the most successful and certainly attractive early diesel railcar developments by the pre-nationalisation private railway companies.

Worcester's railcar allocation remained relatively stable in those last few years of service operations. Railcar W29W was withdrawn several months earlier than the rest in August 1962 and replaced at Worcester by W24W. It has to be said that official and semi-official allocation records in some cases conflict and did not altogether reflect the practical situation on the ground in the final years. Photographic evidence and local observers have confirmed twin railcars W33/38W worked out of Worcester during that final period, although some official and semi-official records incorrectly show them as allocated to Reading when withdrawn in August 1962. This pair remained prominently stored outside Worcester's railcar servicing depot for some considerable time after withdrawal.

Ex-GWR Diesel Railcars – Worcester
Last Operational Depot on the Western Region
Official Allocation at Time of Final Withdrawal – October 1962

W20W W22W	W23W W24W	W26W W32W Total: 6

Great Western Days as diesel railcar No 6 in its original chocolate and cream livery pauses between trips at Great Malvern in 1937. It was delivered new to Worcester in September 1935 and would spend its whole working life there until withdrawal in April 1958. RAIL ON-LINE

Railcar W22W 'painted in later BR mid-green livery' is stabled at Worcester on its day of rest, Sunday 26 June 1960. W22W was delivered new to Newport in September 1940 and had two spells at Worcester, the final one being from 1957 to October 1962 withdrawal. It was one of six final Worcester based class members withdrawn as the class passed into history. Fortunately W22W was rescued for preservation by the Great Western Society at Didcot. N. FIELDS. MANCHESTER LOCOMOTIVE SOCIETY

Railcar W32W in BR carmine and cream livery that suited them well, standing outside the Worcester railcar servicing shed on 10 June 1956. The railcars occupied the first two roads of the wagon repairs shop, the remaining roads still used for wagon repairs. W32W entered service at Llanelly in February 1941 and had reached Worcester by 1950. It worked from there until October 1962 withdrawal at the end of the railcar era. N. FIELDS. MANCHESTER LOCOMOTIVE SOCIETY

Railcar W32W leaving Bewdley for Tenbury Wells and Woofferton on 24 September 1955. The driver rather precariously hangs out of his cab window ready to pick up the single line token from the signalman stood trackside by the crossover. Just out of view is the branch junction, whilst the main Severn Valley route will continue straight ahead. A high proportion of both route's services were ex-GWR railcar worked with vehicles and their drivers coming from Worcester daily. F.W. SHUTTLEWORTH. ANDREW SMITH COLLECTION

Tenbury Wells station with a diesel railcar service from Bewdley to Woofferton having just come to a stand. The guard is about to alight whilst three ladies meeting the train and several station staff look on. It appears several parcels on the four wheeled barrow will shortly be loaded on to the service. MANCHESTER LOCOMOTIVE SOCIETY

Woofferton with a diesel railcar service from Bewdley on the main line platform. The station sign proudly announces 'Woofferton Junction for Tenbury Wells and Bewdley', although public and working timetables referred to this otherwise wayside station simply as Woofferton. DAVE WALDREN

Malvern Link. An unidentified diesel railcar runs into Malvern Link on the Worcester to Hereford main line with a local passenger service. The station facilities and platform canopy are generous, despite the presence of Great Malvern station just one and a half miles down the line. M. HALE. GREAT WESTERN TRUST

Railcar W20W gets away from Great Malvern towards Worcester with a local passenger service in c1960. W20W had been delivered new to Newport in June 1940, arriving in Worcester in 1955 from where it worked until October 1962 withdrawal. Yet another of the final railcar batch to meet its end. TIM FAREBROTHER

Fladbury 'between Evesham and Worcester on the Cotswolds main line' was another station that regularly saw Worcester's ex-GWR railcars. Here one pauses there in c1958 whilst the guard checks from the open door for any passengers. The railcars worked quite diverse diagrams and a trip off the Cotswolds line could easily be followed by one to Malvern or Bromyard. STEVE BARTLETT COLLECTION

Railcar W26W standing at Hartlebury on the main line from Worcester to Kidderminster ready to depart with a branch service for Bewdley. The station sign proudly boasts Hartlebury junction for the Severn Valley. This was one of the main access points for Worcester railcars onto the Severn Valley system at the beginning of the day. M. HALE. GREAT WESTERN TRUST

Burlish Halt 'on the line from Hartlebury to Bewdley' opened on 31 March 1930, following the GWR policy of creating new minor stations to combat bus competition. It was of concrete panel construction with a delightful pagoda style bus shelter. Worcester railcar No W26W calls there on 4 July 1959. The halt would close along with the withdrawal of passenger services over the line in January 1970. M. HALE. GREAT WESTERN TRUST

The Sub-Sheds – Evesham, Kingham, Honeybourne and Ledbury

Worcester had historically been responsible for three sub-sheds at Evesham, Honeybourne and Kingham; all located along the Cotswolds line from Worcester to Oxford. A fourth, Ledbury, between Hereford and Worcester, became an additional responsibility in February 1960. It had previously been a Hereford sub-shed then moving under Worcester's control. Each of the depots had very specific and different local duties within their immediate areas.

EVESHAM

EVESHAM SHED

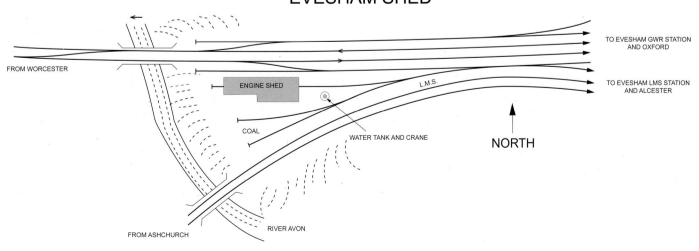

DRAWING - R.SODDY

Evesham Shed
with the line from
Worcester to
Paddington curving
in from the right
hand side. The single
road shed pictured in
c1958 looks in need
of some attention,
which would never
happen, whilst the
two sidings contain
a 4F prairie 2-6-2T
and locomotive coal
wagon. The ex-GWR
parachute style water
tower serves the
shed roads on either
side. M. HALE. GREAT
WESTERN TRUST

The first sub-shed along the Cotswolds route, fourteen miles out of Worcester, was at Evesham. It was located on the down side of the main line from Worcester approaching Evesham and immediately after crossing the River Avon. The former LMS (Midland Railway) line from Birmingham to Ashchurch, via Redditch, passed along the back of the shed site. This then swung south-west before crossing the River Avon and turning due south towards Ashchurch. There it joined the ex-Midland Railway main line from Derby to Bristol. The small former Midland Railway shed at Evesham had closed in 1931.

Evesham's ex-GWR single road shed dated from 1901. It was brick built with a

slated roof topped by smoke ventilators and measured 110ft x 20ft with doors at either end. The line out of the rear of the shed ended at a stop block with a steep drop into the River Avon beyond. The shed floor was blue engineering brick with a locomotive inspection pit running its full length. Outside the shed entrance was another shorter inspection pit. A small office building was attached to the side away from the main line containing a staff mess room and stores. The mess room included wall mounted staff notice boards and a telephone for contacting the signal box or Worcester shed. There was an outside toilet around the back.

Two short sidings fanned out on the far side of the shed building.

These were used for coal wagon storage and further engine stabling. A water column, topped by a parachute style water storage tank, was located between the shed road and the first stabling siding. A small coal brazier with a tall narrow chimney, the latter positioned under the water column feeder, provided rudimentary cold weather precautions. There were no coaling facilities as such and no evidence of coal piles on the ground. Coaling was probably undertaken by hand direct from wagons to locomotive bunkers.

The depot barely survived into the period covered by this book, being closed in June 1961. We do know that for most of the 1950s there were five engines based here, along with ten sets of footplate crews. There was also a shed man on permanent nights for engine servicing and preparation. In the early 1950s, the allocation was headed by a Churchward 4MT 4300 2-6-0 tender engine, but later more usually a Collett 3MT 2251 0-6-0 or BR Standard 2MT 78000 2-6-0. There were additionally in the early 1950s three or four 3F Collett 5700 or 4F Hawksworth 9400 0-6-0PTs based here. An official depot locomotive return in July 1958 and another in October 1960, less than a year before shed closure, showed a reduced allocation of one 2MT BR Standard 78000 2-6-0 and two 3F Collett 5700 0-6-0PTs.

Some records of Sunday shed visits have survived, when most home based engines would have been in residence, and were a further indication of depot numbers. On 29 April 1956 there was one class 2251 0-6-0 and two 0-6-0 pannier tanks on shed, whilst on Sunday 17 May 1956 there was one class 2251 0-6-0 and no less than four 5700 and 9400 0-6-0PTs squeezed on to the cramped site. On Sunday 26 June 1960, barely a year before depot closure, one class 2251 0-6-0, one class 8100 2-6-2T and a 5700 0-6-0PT were in residence.

Douglas Carver, an Evesham fireman from 1954 to 1960, recalled that in the mid-1950s the footplate crew turns with the locomotive class worked, with minor year to year variations, were (LE – light engine):

1. Class 2251 off shed 5.30am. LE to Honeybourne to work freight trip back to Evesham, then shunt up and down yards. LE back to Honeybourne and change footplates with a Honeybourne crew. Crew then took to a fresh engine working the Honeybourne to Worcester pick-up freight as far as home depot Evesham where they were relieved by a Worcester crew.

2. Class 5700 or 9400 off shed 5.45am. LE to Evesham carriage sidings and draw out stock for 7.03 and 8am passenger services. LE to Honeybourne to form No5 banking engine, then 12 noon LE to Evesham for relief.

3. Class 5700, 9400 or 5101 off shed 5.45am. Work 7.03am Evesham - Leamington Spa passenger, returning with 9.15am passenger to Evesham. Next work 11.05am Evesham - Leamington Spa, returning with 1.05pm local passenger to Evesham.

4. Class 4300 off shed 6am. Work 8.03am Evesham - Birmingham Moor St. passenger as far as Stratford-upon-Avon. Engine and crew came off there, next working 8.45am Stratford-upon-Avon - Leamington Spa, returning with 11.20am Leamington Spa-Evesham-Worcester Shrub Hill. Relieved at Evesham by fresh Evesham crew.

5. Class 5700 or 9400 off shed 6.45am. Shunt Evesham LMS yard and work trips between LMS and Western yards all morning until relieved by Evesham crew.

6. On duty 12.30pm. Relieve Turn 2 off returned Honeybourne No5 banking engine. Shunt Evesham up and down yard and Midland exchange sidings until relieved at 8pm by Turn 8.

7. On duty 1pm. Relieve Turn 4 on 11.20am Leamington Spa-Evesham-Worcester Shrub Hill worked by Class 4300. Return with 4.27pm Worcester Foregate St.-Stratford-upon-Avon-Leamington Spa as far as Stratford-upon-Avon. Relieved there by Evesham crew off 4.09pm Evesham-Stratford-upon-Avon. Change engines and work the 5.30pm Birmingham Moor Street-Evesham passenger forward from Stratford-upon-Avon. Then engine to shed and dispose.

8. On duty 1.30pm. Relieve Turn 5 on Evesham Midland shunt engine until engine to shed 7pm. Relieve Turn 6 on afternoon Evesham shunting engine until end of shift. Loco to shed.

9. On duty 1.45pm. Relieve Turn 3 on arrival of 1.05pm Leamington Spa-Evesham, berth stock and engine to shed and service. Same engine to station to work 4.09pm Evesham - Stratford-upon-Avon. Change footplates with Turn 7 on 4.27pm from Worcester Foregate St. and work 5.45pm Stratford-upon-Avon-Leamington Spa. Then work 7.20pm Leamington Spa-Stratford-upon-Avon. Recess there until work 10.45pm Stratford-upon-Avon-Evesham. Engine to shed.

Some of this work had clearly been lost by July 1958, when Evesham's allocation was down to one 2MT BR Standard 78000 2-6-0 and two 5700 0-6-0PTs. It remained at that reduced level until depot closure in June 1961. Despite the somewhat involved footplate crew and

engine workings for such a small depot, a closer look at the work content reveals how vulnerable it actually was to future loss of work. The local passenger service to Stratford-upon-Avon and Leamington Spa would succumb to DMU operation around 1961, whilst the local freight and banking assistance given in the Honeybourne area could easily have been covered from that depot, which would remain open until December 1965. Any duties left over would have been relatively easily integrated into Worcester turns.

One identifiable steam working that remained after depot closure was the Evesham shunt engine. The goods yard would remain an important loading point for Vale of Evesham perishables and other traffic. One of Worcester's 204hp diesel mechanical (later class 03) shunting engines would in future be out-based here. A September 1961 footplate return showed a small link of four drivers still booking on at Evesham, principally to cover the shunting pilot duties.

A notable steam-hauled survivor after depot closure was Evesham's long distance commuting service, by then a slightly amended 8am Evesham to Birmingham Snow Hill, returning as a 5.45pm Birmingham Snow Hill to Evesham. Locomotive provision for the round trip became a Worcester 5MT 'Hall' or 'Grange' 4-6-0 working through to Birmingham instead of as previously changing engines at Stratford-upon-Avon. At times a Worcester 4MT BR Standard 75000 4-6-0 or 4MT 2-6-2T would substitute and even one of the depot's 7P 'Castle' 4-6-0s could appear. Latter examples working the morning service were Worcester's No 7009 *Athelney Castle* on 7 July 1962, No 7023 *Penrice Castle* on 23 May 1964 and No 7005 *Sir Edward Elgar* on 4 July 1964.

Evesham Shed containing engines on their day of rest, Sunday 29 April 1956. Outside are Worcester's 4F 0-6-0PT No 9429, an unidentified 3MT 2251 class 0-6-0 and 3F 0-6-0PT No 7750. An interesting minor detail is the coal brazier with an extended metal chimney providing rudimentary winter weather protection for the ex-GWR parachute style water tower. R.C. RILEY. TRANSPORT TREASURY

River Bridge Renewal at Evesham on 7 June 1959 with the shed in the background. Guy Kerry, Bert Humphries and Don Green watch proceedings whilst the two R&M department 45 tons Ransome & Rapier cranes in use are on the left Wolverhampton Stafford Road's No 17 and on the right Swindon Works No 19. BRIAN PENNEY

Evesham Shed
pictured in the 1940s appearing much the same as in later photographs other than the locomotives on view. Also noteworthy is the delightful GWR gas lamp standard which has been replaced in later images by an electric light attached to the telephone pole. Resting outside the shed is a Dean Goods 0-6-0 and 2-6-2 prairie tank No 4558. W.A. Camwell. Manchester Locomotive Society

8am Evesham to Birmingham Snow Hill commuter train, via Stratford-upon-Avon, nears Bearley on 23 May 1964. The diagrammed Worcester 5MT 'Hall' 4-6-0 has today been substituted by more impressive 7P 4-6-0 No 7023 *Penrice Castle*. Once an Evesham shed turn, with more humble locomotive provision, Worcester had taken responsibility for the service since Evesham's June 1961 depot closure. Gerald T. Robinson

KINGHAM

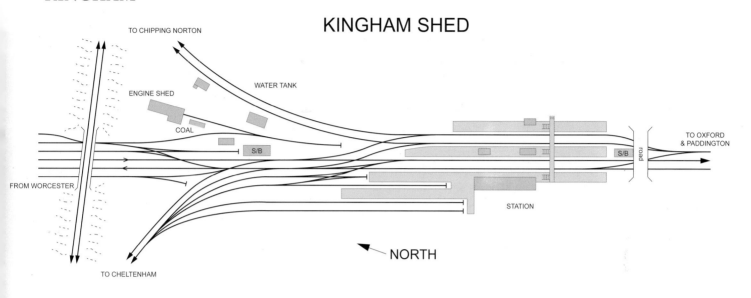

KINGHAM SHED

TO CHIPPING NORTON

WATER TANK

ENGINE SHED

COAL

S/B

FROM WORCESTER

TO CHELTENHAM

STATION

TO OXFORD & PADDINGTON

road

S/B

NORTH

DRAWING - R.SODDY

Kingham Shed viewed through the signals on the down main at the Worcester end of the station. The Chipping Norton branch can be seen curving away to the right of the shed, whilst to the left the lower of the pair of main signals leads towards the Cheltenham branch. The grounded old coach body in front of the shed is worth noting and no doubt had a story to tell. It's late afternoon on 2 July 1962 and 2MT 2-6-0 No 78001's work is done for the day. BEN ASHWORTH

Further along the Cotswolds line was Kingham, thirty-six miles from Worcester and twenty-one miles from Oxford. In 1960, it still was the junction for branch lines to Chipping Norton and Cheltenham, both still having local passenger services. It was also a principal calling point for Hereford-Worcester-Paddington expresses. The Kingham to Chipping Norton branch had originally run through to Kings Sutton, on the main line into Banbury. Passenger services beyond Chipping Norton had been withdrawn in 1951. A short cut-off linking the Chipping Norton and Cheltenham branches crossed over the main line on the Worcester side of Kingham station. This had enabled through running between both local routes without reversal at Kingham but was latterly rarely used and taken out of use in 1960. It dated from 1906, as did a third side of a triangle at Hatherley Junction, Cheltenham. These had together enabled through running for an early 1900s daily express passenger service from Newcastle and Hull to Swansea, via the Great Central, Banbury, Gloucester and Barry. It was known as the 'Ports to Ports Express'.

Kingham's small engine shed, dating from 1913, was a brick built single road building. It had a slated roof topped by smoke ventilators. A shed office and stores was built into the side. The shed measured 75ft x 20ft and the office section an additional 20ft x 15ft. A pair of wooden doors was provided but rarely used. A standard GWR water column was located immediately outside along with a wooden footplate level coaling platform. An old grounded coach body was positioned between the shed and the signal box and may have had a depot function. Locomotives leaving the shed drew forward towards a head shunt, then they set back towards the up sidings before another reversal there to gain the main line. The depot had been originally built with a small turntable later removed.

For many years, a single elderly 'Dean Goods' 0-6-0 had been the regular depot resident. This rotated between Worcester's 1894 built 'Dean Goods' No 2339, 1895 built No 2458 or 1897 built No 2551. The retention of these elderly steeds had been dictated by the route restrictive Moreton-in-Marsh to Shipston-on-Stour branch. Replacement motive power arrived at Worcester in July 1953 in the form of recently built BR Standard 2MT 2-6-0s Nos 78008 and 78009, joined by No 78001 in May 1954. One of these was regularly out-based at Kingham until December 1962 depot closure.

A September 1961 footplate return showed an establishment of just two drivers and two firemen, one of the latter a vacancy. There was also a coalman responsible for locomotive preparation and servicing. In late 1960, the single engine diagram comprised (LE: light engine):

1. Off shed 6.10am, shunting as required. Work 7.10am Kingham-Chipping Norton arr. 7.22am mixed passenger and freight. Return with 8.10am Chipping Norton-Kingham arr. 8.20am mixed passenger and freight. Next work 8.38am Kingham-Moreton-in-Marsh passenger (not school holidays), return 9.10am LE to Kingham (the single passenger coach returned on the following Worcester worked freight trip). Next worked 10.30am MWFO Kingham-Chipping Norton freight trip arr. 10.45am. Shunt and return 1pm MWFO Chipping Norton-Kingham freight trip arr. 1.15pm and to shed.

The Moreton-in-Marsh to Shipston-on-Stour branch had been opened in July 1889 along the route of an earlier tramway. The sharp curves of the latter alignment made it a slow and restrictive route. Passenger services had been withdrawn in July 1929 and goods traffic would follow in May 1960. Branch servicing had fitted easily into the locomotive diagram described as a 9.15am TTho Moreton-in-Marsh to Shipston-on-Stour arr. 10.32am, returning as an 11.10am to Moreton-in-Marsh arrive 12.23pm, then1.50pm LE to Kingham and to shed. No additional work replaced this gap in the locomotives' day on Tuesdays and Thursdays after the service was withdrawn. No identifiable work can be found for a late turn duty despite the 1961 footplate establishment return showing two sets of footplate crews being based here. Looked at realistically, the Kingham arrangements were never the most economic use of resources.

The six branch passenger trains a day between Cheltenham and Kingham were all worked by Cheltenham 4MT 4500 or 5101 2-6-2Ts, returning with a balanced working after a short turnaround at Kingham. There were only two passenger services a day between Kingham and Chipping Norton. The morning 7.10am was worked by the Kingham engine as previously described, followed by a 4pm to Chipping Norton and return worked by the engine and stock off an afternoon Cheltenham service during its Kingham layover. The branch freight trip from Cheltenham to Kingham was also an out and back working from the Cheltenham end. Similarly the daily freight trip from Worcester to Kingham and return was worked out and back by a Worcester engine and crew. The Kingham based engine therefore had minimum involvement in this busy junction activity.

Kingham Station. Worcester 'Castle' 4-6-0 No 7007 *Great Western* prepares to depart with the 3.15pm Paddington to Hereford on 2 July 1962. Meanwhile Cheltenham's 4MT 2-6-2T No 4101 has just completed a round trip to Chipping Norton. Having run around its stock it will shortly make a propelling movement before returning into the station to form the 5.15pm branch line service to Cheltenham. BEN ASHWORTH

Kingham shed would close in December 1962 following the 15 October 1962 withdrawal of passenger services between Kingham and Chipping Norton and between Cheltenham and Kingham. This included the complete closure of the latter line between Cheltenham and Bourton-on-the-Water (exclusive). About this time, the 8.38am Kingham to Moreton-in-Marsh schools train was also withdrawn. This just left the local freight tripping work after depot closure which became a Worcester responsibility. The new more efficient arrangements, which were virtually unchanged in the June 1964 timetable, consisted of a Worcester 4MT 5101 2-6-2T and crew working a 7.25am Worcester Yard to Kingham arr. 10.29am, returning as a 2.25pm Kingham to Worcester Yard arr. 7.33pm. The return journey included a 5.10 to 6.45pm extended period at Evesham to shunt and pick up traffic. A fresh Worcester crew relieved the turn part way through the day. During the late morning Kingham layover the trip serviced Bourton-on-the-Water MWFO and Chipping Norton TThSO. Goods facilities were withdrawn from Bourton-on-the-Water from 7 September 1964, but Chipping Norton would survive for some years longer.

Chipping Norton. Cheltenham's 4MT 2-6-2T No 5514 waits to return to Kingham in the late 1950s with the afternoon return round trip before working a branch line service back to Cheltenham. M. HALE. GREAT WESTERN TRUST

Kingham Shed. Worcester's BR Standard 2MT 2-6-0 No 78001 rests on shed on Boxing Day 26 December 1960. One of these small tender engines was a constant presence at Kingham, rotating between Worcester's Nos 78001, 78008 and 78009. G. SHUTTLEWORTH. MANCHESTER LOCOMOTIVE SOCIETY

Kingham Freight Trip. Rounding the curve into Kingham, with the shed in the background, is 4MT 2-6-2T No 5152 with the 12.30pm freight trip from Chipping Norton in 1963. Despite still carrying a Wolverhampton Stafford Road shed plate, the engine had been transferred from there to Worcester in November 1962. Kingham shed had closed in December 1962 and the area was now served by a 7.25am Worcester Yard to Kingham freight trip that then serviced Bourton-on-the-Water MWFO and Chipping Norton TThSO before returning as a 2.25pm Kingham to Worcester Yard. F.A. HAYNES

Shipston-on-Stour's long closed station on 15 December 1960; seven months after the branch from Moreton-in-Marsh had finally closed to freight. The station however had not seen a passenger train since service withdrawal in July 1929. ROY DENISON

Stretton-on-Fosse was the intermediate station between Moreton-in-Marsh and Shipston-on-Stour. This misty atmospheric scene taken on 15 December 1960 depicts the station that had not seen a passenger service since July 1929. Now not even the twice weekly freight trip would disturb the peaceful scene. ROY DENISON

HONEYBOURNE

Honeybourne Locomotive Stabling Siding with Worcester's 3MT 0-6-0 No 2289 between duties on 26 June 1960. The engine is carrying No2 pilot target on the buffer beam which covered up yard shunting and banking duties as required. K. Fairey/Colourrail

Honeybourne was the third Worcester sub-shed along the Cotswolds line, nineteen miles from Worcester and five miles beyond Evesham. A village with a population of barely 1,600, it had a passenger station at which only local services called. It did however have a more important freight role, with up and down shunting yards and freight recessing loops on both sides of the main line. The track layout and sidings accommodation had been extended following the 1906 completion of the new GWR route from Cheltenham to Honeybourne. From here, the latter used the existing but enhanced local route to Stratford-upon-Avon. By 1908, these works had been completed, along with the opening of the North Warwickshire line from Bearley Junction to Tyseley. Taken together, these created a new GWR double track main line from Cheltenham to the Birmingham area. The new route passed under the Cotswolds main line on the Oxford side of Honeybourne. The latter did not have a passenger station on the new line but did have access to it in both directions by a new triangular junction. This included a new local passenger service from Cheltenham that mostly terminated at Evesham. The freight yard at Honeybourne was further expanded in 1942 to deal with increased wartime traffic.

HONEYBOURNE JUNCTIONS

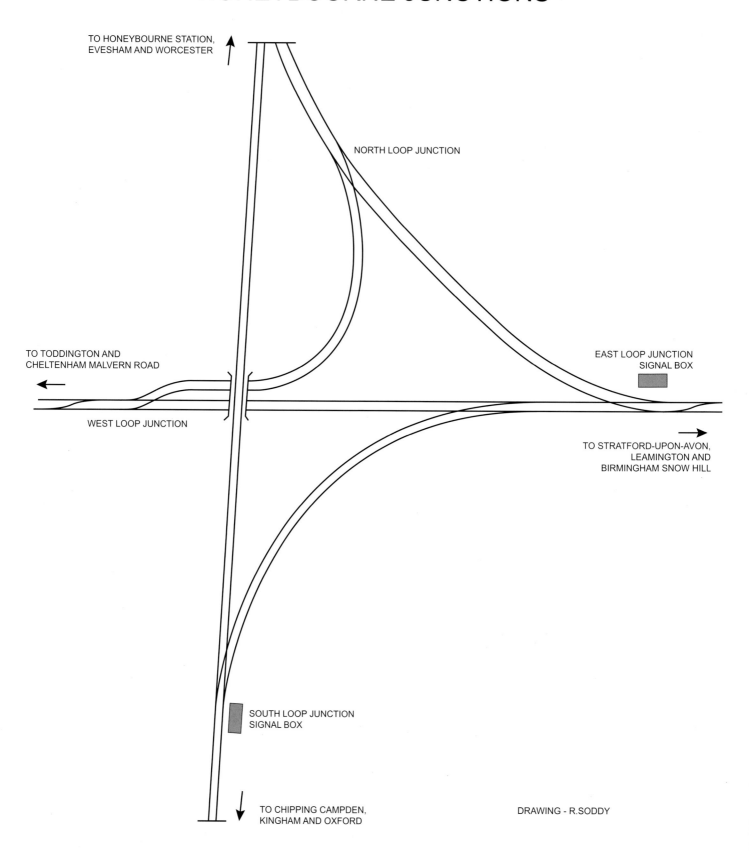

TO HONEYBOURNE STATION,
EVESHAM AND WORCESTER

NORTH LOOP JUNCTION

TO TODDINGTON AND
CHELTENHAM MALVERN ROAD

EAST LOOP JUNCTION
SIGNAL BOX

WEST LOOP JUNCTION

TO STRATFORD-UPON-AVON,
LEAMINGTON AND
BIRMINGHAM SNOW HILL

SOUTH LOOP JUNCTION
SIGNAL BOX

TO CHIPPING CAMPDEN,
KINGHAM AND OXFORD

DRAWING - R.SODDY

The real justification for the small motive power and footplate staff out-base here was the need to bank freight trains up Campden Bank towards Oxford. Honeybourne was located at the start of the steepest section of the climb and assistance was provided for most Oxford and London area bound freight trains. This was usually from Honeybourne to Chipping Campden, with the banking engine loose coupled at the rear, dropping away at the latter point. However, assistance could be requested for an ailing engine or by a nervous driver for the extended section from Evesham to Moreton-in-Marsh. In this case, the banking engine had to be coupled at the rear. The ruling gradient was 1 in 126 for the last three quarters of a mile approaching Honeybourne from the Worcester direction. It then levelled out through the station area before steepening to 1 in 100 for the next four and a half miles up to Chipping Campden; the final section being through the smoke filled Campden tunnel.

Honeybourne's original wooden engine shed building had been demolished in 1907 to make way for the extended yard track layout. A new shed, also of wooden construction, was built in 1909 but burnt down two years later. They were both located on the upside at the Evesham end of the layout close to the platform. The shed building was not replaced and instead locomotives were kept on what was little more than a stabling siding. This did have the basics of a servicing point, being provided with a small wooden coaling platform protected by a corrugated iron awning and a short locomotive inspection pit. Basic footplate staff accommodation was also provided. Probably the most important feature that gave the stabling point the status of a depot was a surprisingly large footplate establishment. In September 1961, twelve drivers, twelve firemen (one a vacancy)

and two fire droppers were based here. These worked around the clock on banking, shunting, local freight trips and the occasional relief of longer distance freight trains.

The absence of a formal shed building seemed to raise doubts from time to time within officialdom as to the status of Honeybourne and whether it should be classed as a sub-shed or just an out-based stabling point. A surviving October 1958 official BR 87329 booklet, an internal publication listing all BR engine sheds in the same format as used in Ian Allan locomotive shed books, raised doubts surrounding Honeybourne's status. Listed under 85A Worcester was just Evesham and Kingham as its sub-sheds, with no mention of Honeybourne. Likewise, the omission is replicated in all editions of Ian Allan locomotive booklets from the earliest edition in 1955 I have up to 1960. Honeybourne does however begin to appear from the spring 1961 edition of Ian Allan publications through to its December 1965 depot closure.

Frustratingly, it is equally difficult to determine Honeybourne's out-based locomotive allocation. Anyone with memories of passing through Honeybourne in those far off days might typically have seen a 5700 0-6-0PT shunting in the yard, possibly a 3MT 2251 0-6-0 forming up a freight trip and quite definitely at least one 2251 0-6-0 simmering on banking duties. However, Worcester's surviving official monthly locomotive workload returns between January 1963 and April 1965 show just one engine out-based at Honeybourne and it is on banking duties. Even more confusingly, this is shown to be a BR Standard 4MT 75000 4-6-0 between January 1963 and January 1964 and only then a 3MT 2251 0-6-0 from February 1964 onwards. However, surviving photographic evidence throughout the period consistently shows 2251s as the locomotives of choice on banking duties.

Perhaps local Worcester practice was at variance with official published locomotive diagrams. The use of 2251 0-6-0s ceased after May 1965, when Worcester's last class members Nos 2222 and 2244 were withdrawn. After that date Worcester increasingly sent out whatever was available for banking duties, although BR Standard 4MT 75000 4-6-0 were the locomotive of choice.

Having studied contemporary freight working timetables and the limited locomotive diagram information available, it becomes clearer why records tend to only show one engine permanently out-based here. A number of relevant locomotive diagrams started the day light engine from either Evesham's sub-shed, until that closed in June 1961, or from Worcester itself. These then formed local duties at Honeybourne, including the essential banking duties. Typically, in the winter 1960/61 timetable there was a 5.45am light engine from Evesham to Honeybourne, worked by an Evesham footplate crew, that then worked a 6.06am Honeybourne to Evesham freight trip. The engine and Evesham crew then returned light engine to Honeybourne, where they exchanged footplates with a Honeybourne crew who made use of that engine for the rest of the day. Similarly, there was a 6.15am light engine from Worcester to Honeybourne, worked by a Worcester crew. Worcester fireman Mick Rock recalls that on arrival at Honeybourne they would exchange footplates with a Honeybourne crew on another 2251 class 0-6-0 that needed returning to Worcester for servicing. The fresh engine at Honeybourne would then perform banking duties for the rest of the day. Meanwhile, the Worcester crew returned home with the former Honeybourne engine as a 9.30am local freight trip to Worcester. There was a third light engine movement at 6.25am from Evesham to Honeybourne. It then worked an 8.30am (TFO) pick-up

freight to Cheltenham or alternatively a 9.15am (MWThO) pick-up freight to Long Marston. With the closure of Evesham shed in June 1961 Honeybourne crews would have picked up some of Evesham's workload along with increased locomotive provision direct from Worcester. The comparatively large size of Honeybourne's footplate establishment is explained by the regular relief of incoming engines for local duties as well as the previously mentioned occasional relief of longer distance freight services.

By 1965, both the importance of the yard and the number of freight trains requiring banking assistance was reducing. Honeybourne fireman Chris Smith recalls that there were now just six sets of footplate staff based there working five regular daily turns with the sixth set for rest day, annual leave and staff sickness. Three of these sets worked around the clock on the banking engine. A fourth set worked a Neath to Swindon freight between Honeybourne and Oxford. A fifth set travelled in to Worcester to collect an engine and work the 1.25am Worcester to Leamington pick-up freight. They returned with a 5.36am Leamington to Evesham local freight, being relieved at Honeybourne by a Worcester crew.

By September 1965, dieselisation and further reductions in main line freight services saw the banking engine being only occasionally used. A reduced Honeybourne footplate establishment carried on until the end of December 1965, coincidental with Worcester's steam depot closure. In saying farewell to this small but once key depot, it is worth recording the extent of its banking duties in busier times. Winter 1960/61 freight trains passing through Honeybourne and climbing Campden Bank are set out in the following table. The symbol 'AE' signifies those scheduled to receive banking assistance.

UP FREIGHT TRAIN SERVICES – WINTER 1960/61 TIMETABLE
HONEYBOURNE - BANK ENGINE DUTIES
Note AE: Stops for banking assistance

Honeybourne	Honeybourne Junction South	Train Details – Mondays to Saturdays
AM	**AM**	
12.26/12AE29 MX		8A09 11.35pm Worcester Yard–Paddington
	12.28/01AE05 MX	7O06 5.25pm Spandon–Fawley (Oil Train)
	01.53/01AE57 MX	10.15pm Oxley–Westbury
	02.32/02AE36 MX	6A06 12.45pm Bordesley–Moreton Cutting
02.24/02AE55 MX		8A22 7.35pm Pontypool Road–Yarnton
	05.10/05AE39 MX	5O06 3.25am Oxley–Basingstoke
04.52/05AE35 MX		7A16 11.45pm Rogerstone–Yarnton
06.01/06AE04 MX		6V07 1.35am Crewe–Reading West Junction
06.06/06AE10 MO		7A16 12.50am Rogerstone–Yarnton, via Ashchurch & Evesham
08.24/09.30 Daily		9B88 6.35am Worcester Yard–Kingham, to be regulated TuO to follow 4B38
09.10/09.30 TuO		4B38 2.45am Croes Newydd–Swindon
10.25/10AE38 Daily		8A55 11.40am Neath–Yarnton via Ashchurch & Evesham
PM	**PM**	
11.53/12AE03 Daily		8A65 5.10am Pontypool Road–Yarnton
12.25/12AE35 Daily		5A57 9.30am Oxley–Moreton Cutting
2.24/2AE37 SX		7A40 8.20am Cardiff–Yarnton via Ashchurch & Evesham
6.10/7.40 SX		8A64 3.30pm Worcester Yard–Paddington
6.44/7.25 SO		8A64 5pm Worcester Yard–Paddington
8pm Passing time MX		4V32 3.15pm Longbridge–Swindon
8.30.8AE37 Daily		7A61 2.45pm Rogerstone–Yarnton via Ashchurch & Evesham
9.25/9.53 Daily		5E09 12.10pm Llandilo Junction–Cambridge. Via Ashchurch & Evesham
10.01/10AE05 SO		7A56 10.40am Aberdare–Yarnton via Ashchurch & Evesham
9.55/10.10 SX		4V72 12.35pm Aintree West–Morris Cowley
	10.23/10AE53 Daily	7V40 6.50pm Washwood Heath–Morris Cowley
	10.51/10AE54 SO	8A21 8.35pm Bordesley Junction–Moreton Cutting or Swindon
10.34/11.05 SX		5A02 10pm Worcester Yard–Paddington
11.14/11AE25 Daily		7A04 6.20pm Cardiff–Yarnton via Ashchurch & Evesham
11.36/11AE45 SO		8A02 10.45pm Worcester Yard - Reading West Junction

Honeybourne Station with Worcester's 3MT 0-6-0 No 2291 pausing between shunting and banking duties on 4 March 1964. A February 1938 build, it had spent the previous four years at Swindon before transferring to Worcester in January 1964. Most of its time would be spent out-based at Honeybourne before its September 1964 withdrawal. R.G. NELSON. TERRY WALSH

Honeybourne Banker 3MT 0-6-0 No 2246 nears the end of the four and a half miles climb from Honeybourne to Chipping Campden as it enters the final section through the half mile long Campden Tunnel on 2 July 1962. BEN ASHWORTH

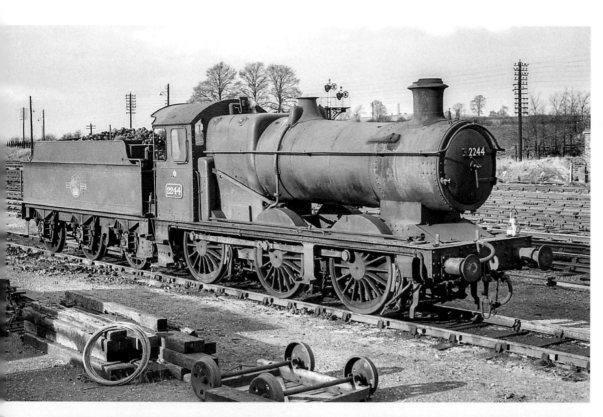

Honeybourne Banking Engine
Worcester's 3MT 0-6-0 No 2244 on 7 November 1964 awaits its next call to assist a freight train up the four and a half miles Campden Bank. By this date there were just two daily turns for these plucky engines, sharing banking duties with short distance freight trips. RICHARD POSTILL

Honeybourne Staff record for posterity the retirement of driver Sidney Page on 1 July 1957. He is on the left and alongside him fireman Ray Hughes, guard Bill Garrett and a local shunter. His final run had been a short trip to Stratford-upon-Avon. No 7818 *Granville Manor* was a Tyseley engine at the time. B. ENGLAND. R. HUGHES

Campden Bank. 8F 2-8-0 No 3823 slogs its way up Campden Bank in spring 1964 with the 11.10pm Neath to Yarnton Yard, routed via Cheltenham Malvern Road and Toddington to Honeybourne. A lengthy layover was booked there whilst the through South Wales engine turned via the Honeybourne junctions. The service was booked to leave Honeybourne at 12.23pm with banking assistance from there, today being provided by 3MT 0-6-0 No 2253. Despite carrying a Severn Tunnel Junction shed plate No 3823 had been transferred to Neath in October 1963. F.A. HAYNES.

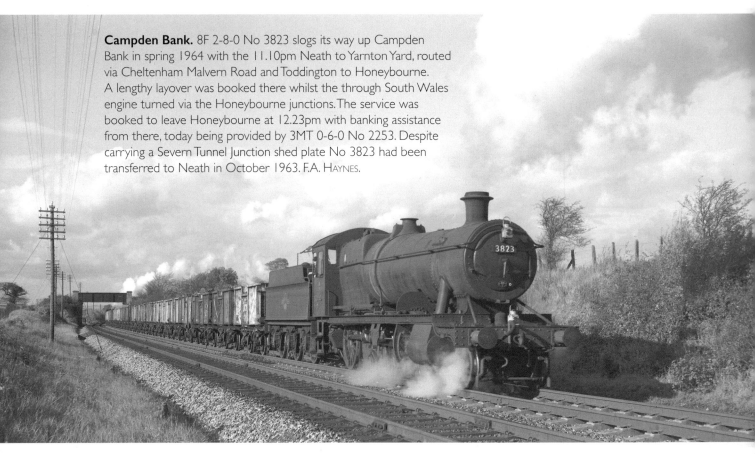

Campden Bank. Worcester's BR Standard 2MT 2-6-0 No 78008 battles up Campden Bank with a lengthy freight train, undoubtedly with banking assistance, during the deep snow of winter 1962/63. The time of day doesn't fit with a Worcester to Kingham freight trip and the load is rather heavy for such a service. It would also be unusual for such an underpowered locomotive to be entrusted with a long distance freight train unless there was a serious locomotive shortage. It is most likely to be a special service during that disrupted heavy snowfall period. F.A. HAYNES

Banking Assistance is provided by a Honeybourne 3MT 2251 class 0-6-0 as train engine Severn Tunnel Junction's 4MT 2-6-0 No 7328 works hard with this loaded coal train for Yarnton or the London area. The picturesque snowy landscape is in the grip of the freezing, snowbound 1962/63 winter that caused severe disruption to the country for many months. F.A. HAYNES

LEDBURY

LEDBURY SHED

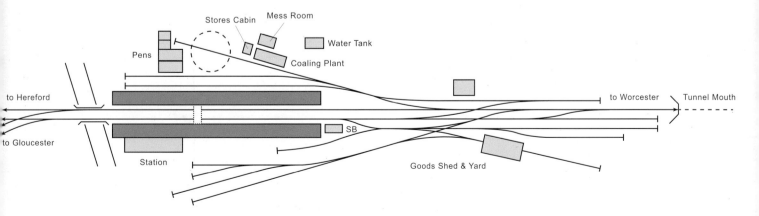

Ledbury Panorama from high above the tunnel mouth looking towards Hereford. The goods yard is to the left, whilst the locomotive stabling point and coaling platform is hidden by hillside immediately to the right of the up platform, wagons occupying the siding alongside. The passenger train has been stood where up freights would pause awaiting banking assistance; the banking engine running light through the station on the opposite line. It would then come onto the rear of the freight train through the crossover that can be seen beyond the station end. Meanwhile Worcester's 4MT 2-6-2T No 6147 pulls away with the 5.45pm Ledbury to Worcester Foregate Street local passenger service on 24 June 1964. BEN ASHWORTH

The market town of Ledbury lies just across the border in Herefordshire and to the west of the Malvern Hills. In 1961, it had a population of 4,250. It was and still is a principal calling point for main line passenger services from Hereford to Worcester, Birmingham and London Paddington.

The route had also been the GWR's principal freight artery from South Wales to the West Midlands and little had changed in the early 1960s. In the winter 1961/62 timetable, there were no less than eighteen freight services daily from South Wales, peaking through Ledbury during the morning and night shifts. Over half started from Pontypool Road's busy marshalling yard, whilst others came from Llandilo Junction, Cardiff and Hereford. A third of them were destined for Stourbridge Junction, where traffic was sorted for onwards destinations, whilst others were for Worcester, Oxley, Bordesley Junction, Soho Pool and Birmingham Lawley Street. A further two were destined for Yarnton yard, near Oxford, travelling from Worcester over the Cotswolds line.

The Hereford to Worcester route was initially gently undulating until noticeably steepening on the approaches to Ledbury. There the rising gradient increased dramatically to 1 in 70/80 through the sulphurous narrow single bore Ledbury Tunnel. Beyond there, the line re-doubled and continued climbing at 1 in 124/148 until Colwall Tunnel was reached. Freight trains, except for the lighter single daily local Worcester pick-up service, were scheduled to receive banking assistance between Ledbury station and Ledbury North, just beyond the end of the tunnel.

Worcester fireman Mick Rock was sent down to cover a Ledbury fireman's turn during staff shortfalls there on several occasions. He would travel down by local passenger train from Worcester to start his shift. He recalls the typical procedure that was followed:

'Freight trains requiring assistance would whistle up for a banker when passing the previous signal box at Stoke Edith. The message was passed on by telephone to the banking crew's cabin at Ledbury. The banker would then move off the stabling point behind the up platform, crossing over to the down main where it would pass through the station to the cross-over located beyond. Once the freight train had come to a stand the banking engine would cross onto the up line and buffer up behind it, although remaining uncoupled for the banking movement. When both locos were ready and the signal cleared whistles would be exchanged. The banker would first ease up the couplings as a powerful and responsive start was needed with the gradient immediately steepening as you entered the tunnel. Trains would be banked as far as Ledbury North signal box at the far end where the banker dropped away and came to a stand. This left the train engine to battle up the remainder of the gradient towards Colwall tunnel. Returning light engine to Ledbury through the same single bore tunnel was not a pleasant experience, as you encountered the still dense smoke from the earlier loaded train movement.'

The story is told of another young Worcester fireman who, having been unwittingly sent down to relieve at Ledbury, spent his first trip sat on the footplate floor with his face covered by a soaking handkerchief as smoke swirled around him. It must have been challenging work, as the crew's only duties were the repeated banking trips through these sulphurous depths on the steeply rising gradient. In an attempt to ease the situation, it was the practice for banking engines, contrary to standard practice, to be smokebox trailing whilst banking to minimise the effect of its own exhaust on the crew. It is however questionable whether this helped much with a hard working train engine up ahead still doing the damage. One has to question the long term health consequences for regular crews.

Ledbury's locomotive servicing facility was located behind the up station platform. There was no actual building, just a stabling siding with a small coaling platform. The latter had a somewhat fragile corrugated iron veranda providing limited weather protection. The stabling siding led to a small but little used turntable dating from 1885. There were two further short sidings between the stabling siding and the station platform, one of which was used for wagons of locomotive coal. Behind and to the left of the coaling platform was a small corrugated iron store or lamp hut and beyond that a relatively modern flat roofed brick built staff mess room with stove-pipe chimney. A telephone linked the mess room with the signal box for banking instructions. A water tank was to be found on higher ground to the rear of the stabling siding feeding water columns at the end of the up and down station platforms.

Ledbury had historically been a sub-shed of Hereford. This changed in February 1960, when the latter's reporting line changed from the Worcester to the Newport Motive Power District. Hereford's shed code consequentially changed from 85C to 86C, the latter having previously been used by Cardiff Canton. A single 8F 5205 2-8-0 tank, a class more commonly found on South Wales colliery services, was out-based at Ledbury. No 5243 had transferred from Hereford to Worcester

with its existing banking workload in February 1960, joined by several others to make a small allocation of three at Worcester. The banking engine was booked to return to Worcester at the end of the week in the early hours of Sunday mornings after, 'The passage of the last up freight train'. I wonder how often a frustrated banking engine crew would be enquiring of the signalman how that last often late running freight service was running. The engine for the following week returned as a 5.15am (MO) light engine from Worcester, later retimed to 6.15am (MO) in the Summer 1963 timetable. In September 1961 there were three drivers and three firemen (one a vacancy) based at Ledbury, which would have been the minimum requirement to cover the three shift banking duties. Any staffing shortfall would be covered by overtime or relief from Worcester.

The 5205 2-8-0Ts finally left Worcester in January 1964, after which a 4MT 5101 or 6100 2-6-2T was usually provided. On Saturday 25 April 1964, I rode behind Hereford's 7P 4-6-0 No 5000 *Launceston Castle* on the 4pm Hereford to Paddington as far as Ledbury. There simmering quietly on the bank engine siding was Worcester's 4MT 2-6-2T No 6140 on duty that day. The sub-shed at Ledbury officially closed in July 1964, although banking duties remained a Worcester turn until December 1964. This suggests engines and probably crews were latterly sent down from Worcester as required. It was around this time that the reducing numbers of freight trains from South Wales to the West Midlands were steadily diverted away from the route and Pontypool Road marshalling yard run down. This, coupled with increasing dieselisation, would eliminate the need for banking assistance and another piece of the local railway scene would pass into history.

UP FREIGHT TRAIN SERVICES – WINTER 1961/62 TIMETABLE
LEDBURY–BANK ENGINE DUTIES
Note AE: Stops for banking engine only

Ledbury	Train Details–Mondays to Saturdays
AM	
12.16/12AE19 MX	7H22 11.35pm Hereford–Bordesley Junction
12.54/12AE57 MX	8H51 9pm Pontypool Road–Stourbridge Junction
1.48/1AE51 MX-Q	8H52 1.05am Hereford–Foley Park Sugar Beet
2.57/3AE10 MX	5H52 12.10am Pontypool Road–Stourbridge Junction
4.11/4AE14 MX	6H60 11.45pm Cardiff–Oxley
5.10/5AE13 MX	5H54 9.15pm Llandilo Junction–Stourbridge Junction
5.52/5AE55 MX	8H45 3am Pontypool Road–Oxley
5.59/6AE02 MO	8H45 2.15am Pontypool Road–Oxley
7.21/7AE24 MX	4H46 1.20am Llandilo Junction–Stourbridge Junction
8.36/8AE39 Daily	8A65 3.40am Pontypool Road–Yarnton
9.47/9AE50 Daily	5M17 6.10am Cardiff–Birmingham Lawley Street
10.50/10AE53 Daily	6H86 6.30am Pontypool Road - Worcester
PM	
1.20/1AE38 MX	8H53 9.45am Pontypool Road–Stourbridge Junction
3.33/3AE36 MX	8H38 10.45am Pontypool Road–Bordesley Junction
3.03/3.36 Daily	8H85 12.55pm Hereford–Worcester Pick-up Freight
9.31/9AE34 Daily	6H42 5pm Cardiff- Oxley
10.00/10AE03 Daily	5M71 6.10pm Cardiff–Soho Pool
11.07/11AE10 SX	8A22 7.45pm Pontypool Road–Yarnton
11.24/11AE27 Daily	8H87 6.50pm Pontypool Road - Worcester

Ledbury Stabling Point with 8F 2-8-0T No 5243, attached to a locomotive coal wagon, simmering away awaiting its next banking duty. The disused turntable was used as a stabling siding extension where the coal wagon was sometimes moved. The brick built corrugated iron clad coaling platform lies behind the locomotive. The scene is dated about 1959 and later photographs show the gas lamp replaced by an electric light mounted on a concrete lamp standard. M. HALE. GREAT WESTERN TRUST

Parent Depot Worcester on Sunday 19 August 1962 with regular and decidedly dirty Ledbury banker 8F 2-8-0T No 5205 taking advantage of its day of rest. It had entered service in June 1923; the first of Collett's modified 5205 class build to add to the existing successful Churchward 1910 designed 4200 class 2-8-0Ts. No 5205 had arrived at Worcester in January 1962 from Newport Ebbw Junction and worked from there until its November 1963 withdrawal. R.C. RILEY. TRANSPORT TREASURY

Ledbury Shed dated around 1962/63 with banking engine 8F 2-8-0T No 5205 in residence. The scene illustrates well the stabling point's sparse facilities with the corrugated iron clad coaling platform behind the engine, the footplate staff cabin with smoking chimney to the rear and stores hut to the left. Also just in view is the brick edging of the small little used turntable. The electric light mounted on a concrete post has replaced the gas lamp in the earlier 1959 photograph. GREAT WESTERN TRUST

Banking Assistance will be required for this freight train from South Wales to the West Midlands on 23 May 1964 as it draws to a stand in Ledbury's up platform. In typically filthy condition, Pontypool Road's 5MT 4-6-0 No 6822 *Manton Grange* is in charge with probably a Hereford or Worcester crew on the footplate. Ledbury's corrugated iron clad coaling platform can just be seen to the right of the engine. GERALD T. ROBINSON

Departing Ledbury with 4MT 2-6-2T No 6140 banking out of view at the rear, is the same service re-starting its journey to the West Midlands, headed by Pontypool Road's 5MT 4-6-0 No 6822 *Manton Grange*. The young fireman looks towards the photographer but will soon be taking preventative measures as the steeply graded and shortly smoke filled single bore Ledbury tunnel is entered. By this date the long serving 8F 5205 class 2-8-0Ts had given way to one of Worcester's out-based 4MT 2-6-2Ts. GERALD T. ROBINSON

Worcester to Oxford – The Cotswolds Route

Most memories of the Oxford and Paddington route over the Cotswolds will inevitably involve scenes of the two hourly Hereford-Worcester-Paddington expresses, hauled by Worcester or Old Oak Common 7P 'Castle' 4-6-0s. However, there was so much more other activity going on along the route. It was a principal freight artery with long distance services from the Midlands and South Wales, via both Hereford and Gloucester, for Oxford and the London area. There was a rather fragmented local passenger service serving intermediate stations. Local freight trips served not only the minor stations but also the better used Pershore, Evesham, Honeybourne, Moreton-in-Marsh and Kingham. These were locations still either contributing originating traffic or junctions serving local lines that still retained freight facilities.

The Cotswolds line left Worcester Shrub Hill in a southerly direction, soon passing Norton Junction where services for the ex-Midland Railway route to Gloucester and Bristol dropped away. The route then swung away through fruit and market gardening country to Pershore and Evesham. Soon Honeybourne was reached,

where a link line dropped down to join the ex-GWR Cheltenham to Stratford-upon-Avon route. Honeybourne was also home to a small sub-shed, for freight banking engines on the steeply graded Campden Bank that stretched ahead. At the summit was the half mile long Campden Tunnel, the route then continuing through Moreton-in-Marsh. Until 1960 there had been a freight only branch line from there to Shipston-on-Stour. Next was Kingham, junction for branch lines to Cheltenham and Chipping Norton. Both were still served by passenger services until 1962. Kingham was a home to another small sub-shed where a single freight and passenger trip engine was based. After leaving Kingham the boundary between the Worcester and London Divisions was reached; the route continuing on to Oxford and London.

The sub-sheds along the route and their duties are covered in a separate chapter. Worcester 'Castles' working the Paddington expresses have already been given plenty of exposure in earlier chapters, so here we will focus on other depot's engines working the Paddingtons and most importantly the wide range of other services that used this scenic route across the Cotswolds.

Worcester Shrub Hill. Old Oak Common's No 7029 *Clun Castle* stands proudly heading the 4.05pm Hereford to Paddington on Saturday 13 July 1963. The 'Hymek' D7000 on the middle road will have brought in the Hereford portion onto the rear of the up platform; the diesel then being released onto the centre road through the mid-platform crossover. The 'Castle's' engine and crew, attached to the starting Worcester portion, would then have set back to couple up to the Hereford portion. All of this, including a final brake test, had to be completed within the ten minutes station allowance. Richard Postill

Wylds Lane. Old Oak Common's No 5040 *Stokesay Castle* is rather generous power for a four coach local service for the Cotswolds line in the early 1960s. The train has just left Shrub Hill and is passing the carriage sidings on the left and Metal Box factory sidings on the right, where plenty of freight traffic is on offer. F.A. Haynes

Norton Halt, three miles out of Worcester, is passed by Eastleigh's BR Standard 9F 2-10-0 No 92239, heading a Rowley Regis to Fawley empty oil tanks train in summer 1963. The photographer's family are interested or is it patient observers? This is a good example of the motive power variety to be seen over the Cotswolds route. F.A. HAYNES

Norton Junction. Old Oak Common's No 4085 *Berkeley Castle* hurries past the junction with the 9.20am Stourbridge Junction to Oxford local service in 1962. This was no doubt a balanced return working for the engine, having hopefully worked into Worcester with a more fitting express passenger service the previous day. F.A. HAYNES

Norton Junction is passed by Oxford's No 6910 *Gossington Hall* with the 3.33pm (SO) Moreton-in-Marsh to Worcester Shrub Hill local service in c1962. The train was formed by the engine and stock off the 1.25pm (SO) Oxford to Moreton-in-Marsh, where it had a 2.28pm to 3.33pm layover. It would have been overtaken there by the 1.15pm Paddington to Hereford. The local service comprising just two coaches was a train of note for local enthusiasts, always producing a 5MT mixed traffic engine from a London area depot. F.A. HAYNES

Stoulton, between Pershore and Norton Junction, is approached by Worcester's 3MT 0-6-0 No 2246 in 1963 with a Honeybourne to Worcester local freight trip. Stoulton's freight yard contains several wagons of local traffic awaiting attention. F.A. HAYNES

Pershore Station, between Worcester and Evesham, with some delightful 'what would now be regarded as vintage' road vehicles on show. The single decker bus in the foreground is intriguingly in British Railways livery with a Western Region fleet number on the side. The Austin A40 Farina in the background, first introduced in 1958, helps to date the photograph. STEVE BARTLETT COLLECTION

Pershore Goods Shed is shunted by Worcester's 4MT 2-6-2T No 4124 on 9 April 1964 whilst pausing with a Honeybourne to Worcester local freight service. R.G. NELSON. TERRY WALSH

Evesham GWR Yard. A busy afternoon scene as two main line engines, both from distant depots, work on their respective freight services. Bristol St Phillip's Marsh 5MT 4-6-0 No 6814 *Enborne Grange* pulls out of the yard with a train of loaded vans, whilst Tyseley's 5MT 4-6-0 No 7918 *Rhose Wood Hall* waits patiently in the up loop to make a shunt. The latter is clearly on a shunting movement as its brake van, instead of being on the rear, is formed second behind the engine. F.A. HAYNES

Evesham Station in a busy scene in the late 1950s, with Cheltenham Malvern Road out-based 1P 0-4-2T No 1427 in the down platform with an auto-train working from Cheltenham, via Honeybourne. Meanwhile in the up platform is a Collett 4MT 2-6-2T with a local passenger service. All this would rapidly change with the Cheltenham auto-service being withdrawn in March 1960 and by the early 1960s, most local services worked by diesel units. M. HALE. GREAT WESTERN TRUST

Freight Interlude Evesham. Gloucester Barnwood's Stanier 8F 2-8-0 No 48172 pauses to take water on Thursday 9 May 1963 with a down freight train. Meanwhile, Gloucester Horton Road's Collett 0-6-0PT No 3745 is busy shunting, having worked in a freight trip from Cheltenham St James, via Honeybourne, to where it will later return. BEN ASHWORTH

Evesham Station. Gloucester Barnwood's BR Standard 5MT 4-6-0 No 73031 eases up to a failed DMU in the station platform in late Spring 1962. The guard trackside gives instructions to the driver, whilst a group of interested railwaymen look on at the far end of the platform. F.A. HAYNES

Evesham. Worcester based ex-GWR diesel railcar No W22W takes a break between local passenger duties in this undated scene. Entering service in September 1940, W22W was one of the final class members to be withdrawn in October 1962. DAVE WALDREN

Campden Bank is climbed by hard working Reading 5MT 4-6-0 No 6953 *Leighton Hall* with a heavy freight train from South Wales to Yarnton yard, near Oxford. Van traffic, a good proportion of which will be vacuum brake fitted, comprises the bulk of the load. Out of sight at the rear is a hard working Honeybourne banking engine. F.A. HAYNES

Excursion Train. Seen climbing Campden Bank in 1962 headed by Hereford's 5MT 4-6-0 No 5952 *Cogan Hall*. The Hereford engine is being given a rare opportunity to stretch its legs beyond Worcester, it more usually being limited to working Hereford portions of Paddington services as far as that point. There would be a Worcester footplate crew in charge as Hereford men didn't sign the road beyond Worcester. F.A. HAYNES

Campden Bank is vigorously climbed by Stanier 8F No 48760, with steam to spare, on an up freight service on 20 August 1964. The train is being banked by a Honeybourne 3MT 2251 class 0-6-0. The train engine is not carrying a shed plate, but was transferred from Llanelly to Neath during that month. F.A. HAYNES

Stoulton is passed by free running Saltley 5MT Black 5 4-6-0 No 45280 with a mixed freight train. The date could be as late as 1965, given the abandoned state of the station goods yard. Through LMR locomotive workings on freight services over the Cotswolds line became increasingly common as the 1960s progressed. Meanwhile, the photographer's young daughter adds human interest to the scene. F.A. HAYNES

Moreton-in-Marsh. Worcester's No 7004 *Eastnor Castle* runs into the up platform in autumn 1960 with what appears to be the 1.50pm Hereford to Paddington express. However, the chalked A83 head code looks a bit faded and may refer to an earlier working. The United Dairies creamery and milk bottling plant is in the background, with rail-borne milk tankers in view. A siding derailment here is featured in the following 'Winter in Worcester and the Cotswolds Route' section. F.A. HAYNES

Kingham. The 3.15pm Paddington to Hereford makes a measured start from Kingham headed by Worcester's No 7025 *Sudeley Castle* on 4 May 1963. The shed site and water tower lie behind the lineside building on the left, whilst a member of the public walks briskly along the track side. It surely wouldn't happen on today's railway. GERALD T. ROBINSON

Winter in Worcester and the Cotswolds Route

The 1962/63 winter was one of the worst on record, with snow arriving on Boxing Day and staying on the ground until March. For the railway, the combination of snow and freezing conditions meant a challenging time. Worcester fireman Mick Rock recalls a particular fifteen hours shift for him and his driver:

'One morning in January 1963 I booked on duty with my driver Charlie Knibb to work the local Worcester to Stoke Works freight. Our engine was Worcester's 3MT 0-6-0 No 2246. On arrival in the yard we were told to return to shed and couple up to the breakdown vans as there had been a milk tank wagon derailed in the milk factory sidings at Moreton-in-Marsh.

'Whilst the gang worked on re-railing we made the decision to turn our engine before the return journey, given the exposed nature of class 2251 0-6-0 cabs when travelling tender first with the low tender providing minimal protection. We informed the signalman we wanted to run light engine to Yarnton Yard, near Oxford, to use the turntable. By now it was around 5pm and we experienced falling snow on the way, deciding against topping up the tender at Charlbury water troughs in case it was frozen and damaged our water scoop. We stopped outside Yarnton signal box and informed the signalman we needed to use the turntable. We were met with the reply, "I think its frozen solid". I can't repeat what was said by my driver Charlie Knibb. Having stabled the engine on a nearby siding we walked through the snow to look at the turntable and sure enough it was frozen solid. We couldn't move it and gave up after fifteen minutes, returning to the warmth of the signal box.

'The signalman then rang Oxford to explain our plight and we suggested continuing to Oxford shed to turn there. However we were told in no uncertain terms that the Oxford area was at a stand, plus it was now snowing heavily at Yarnton.

Charlie then suggested Didcot, but got the same response and by now it was 10pm. There was nothing left but to go back tender first to Moreton-in-Marsh. With no cab storm sheet to protect us from the freezing wind and snow we set off there at a gingerly 20 mph. Reaching the gang we found the milk wagon was re-railed and the breakdown gang in the mess coach around a roaring stove. We were treated to the usual ribald jokes at our escapade and after a well-earned steaming mug of tea set off for Worcester. We travelled at a gingerly 20 mph all the way crouched in the cab, arriving back on shed at around 2am. What a day; but at least we were given the mandatory twelve hour rest before reporting for duty once more.'

When the snow stopped and the sun came out some spectacular photographic conditions were experienced and we celebrate these here. Most are by local photographer F.A. Haynes, who braved the winter on numerous occasions to record these very special scenes.

Ghostly Apparition. Taken two winters after Mick Rock's story, snow plough fitted 3MT 0-6-0 No 2253 moves cautiously on shed at Worcester on 4 March 1965 in a heavy snow storm. It is ready for or has just returned from snow plough duties. Adding to its ghostly appearance, the engine had actually been officially withdrawn the previous week ending 27 February 1965; an instruction that the depot had seemingly yet to implement. R.N. Pritchard

Norton Junction. Worcester's 4MT 2-6-2T No 4113 approaches Norton Junction off the Cotswolds line in the 1962/63 winter with a return freight trip from Honeybourne to Worcester. F.A. Haynes

Stoulton Station. During the worst of the 1962/63 winter, locomotive diagrams inevitably broke down. Here, South Wales based No 5037 *Monmouth Castle* hurries through Stoulton with an afternoon Paddington to Hereford service. The engine is misleadingly carrying its 1A03 previous up working head code for the 6.20am Hereford to Paddington, suggesting it had already worked into Worcester the previous night. Now it was returning to the area a second time, far from its home depot. It had been transferred from Neath to Llanelly in January 1963 in the midst of these disruptions. Meanwhile a wellington clad staff member watches the train pass the adjacent foot crossing that had earlier been cleared of snow. F.A. Haynes

Norton Junction with snow lying all around as Old Oak Common's No 5057 *Earl Waldegrave* takes Norton Junction at speed on 9 January 1963 with the 12.05pm Hereford to Paddington. F.A. HAYNES

Campden Bank. Didcot's 8F 2-8-0 No 2852 working hard up Campden Bank in January 1963 with a return Rowley Regis to Fawley empty tanks train. The required safety barrier wagons are evident behind the engine. Short notice motive power is evident as by this date diesel haulage or at least a BR Standard 9F 2-10-0 would be expected on the service. F.A. HAYNES

Norton Junction. Reading based 'Castle' No 5076 *Gladiator* approaches Norton Junction from Worcester at speed with the 10.05am Hereford to Paddington in March 1963. There's nothing like snow to provide a backdrop for a dramatic photograph and there is little thaw in evidence. F.A. HAYNES

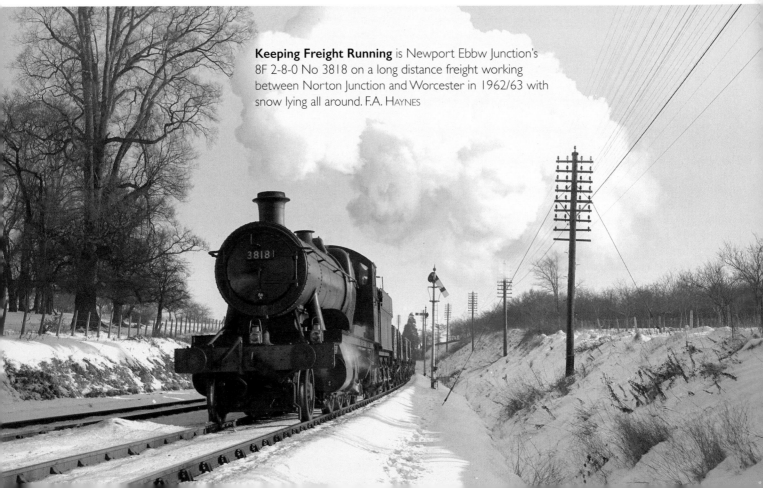

Keeping Freight Running is Newport Ebbw Junction's 8F 2-8-0 No 3818 on a long distance freight working between Norton Junction and Worcester in 1962/63 with snow lying all around. F.A. HAYNES

Campden Bank. Worcester's No 7023 *Penrice Castle* working hard climbing Campden Bank unassisted during the 1962/63 winter with a Hereford to Paddington service. The train should be warm as carriage heating steam wisps from between the third and fourth carriages. The head code is for the 8am Hereford 'The Cathedrals Express', but the photographer recorded it as the 12.05pm Hereford to Paddington. F.A. HAYNES

Worcester to Hereford Route

Trains leaving Worcester Shrub Hill for Hereford took the sharply curved southern side of the Worcester triangle towards Rainbow Hill Junction. There, they joined the route running down the second side of the triangle from Tunnel Junction and the West Midlands towards the city's second principal station, Worcester Foregate Street. Freight trains continued through without stopping and all services headed onwards towards Malvern, Ledbury and Hereford. Some local passenger trains terminated at Malvern or Ledbury, whilst the two hourly expresses from Paddington did so at Hereford. Most cross-country services from Birmingham Snow Hill continued beyond Hereford to Cardiff. The infrequent branch line passenger service to Bromyard had earlier left the main line three miles after Foregate Street at Bransford Road Junction. There were a number of minor halts leaving the city, all opened in the 1920s in an attempt to compete with local bus operation. These included Boughton and Rushwick Halts where I was introduced at a young age to the fascination of railways.

A lot of schools traffic passed between the Malvern area and Worcester, taking boys to the King's School and Royal Grammar School Worcester and the girls to their Grammar School and Alice Ottley School. The return steam-hauled service is well remembered as conveying two coaches for the public and three for the schools; the corridor connection firmly locked between the two sections, although, interestingly, not segregating the boys' and girls' schools' travellers.

The route had also been a major freight artery from South Wales to the West Midlands since former GWR days. Typically, in 1961 there were eighteen up long distance freight services a day passing over the route. Most started from Pontypool Road with thirteen destined for Stourbridge Junction or other West Midlands yards, three for Worcester itself and two for Yarnton, near Oxford. The route was open twenty-four hours a day, with the night hours dominated by the long distance freight services. Once or twice a day a pannier tank hauled local freight trip made its way down from Worcester as far as Malvern Wells.

This varied pattern of services ensured a wide variety of locomotive types to be seen from a surprisingly varied number of motive power depots. Scenes from those far off days bring this delightful thirty miles route section back to life.

Worcester Shrub Hill. Old Oak Common's No 5057 *Earl Waldegrave* has just arrived with the 9.15am Paddington to Hereford on 27 February 1964. It will come off here, returning from Worcester with the 12.05pm Hereford to Paddington after a comparatively tight seventy minutes turnaround. Taking over for Hereford will be a Worcester 'Hall' or 'Grange' 5MT 4-6-0 with a local crew. R.G. NELSON/ TERRY WALSH

Great Malvern. Worcester's No 6856 *Stowe Grange* calls with a Paddington to Hereford service in 1963. The engine was Worcester based from October 1957 to November 1965 withdrawal. Worcester's booked 'Grange' turns were on freight work, but were a regular sight on local passenger duties. RAIL-ONLINE

Colwall Tunnel.
A spectacular view from high above the mouth of the single bore Colwall tunnel. Worcester's No 5971 *Merevale Hall* passes onto the single line, having just passed through Malvern Wells with the 3.15pm Paddington to Hereford on 30 June 1965. This was just six months before the end of Western Region steam operations.
R.N. PRITCHARD

Ledbury Tunnel. Worcester's 4MT 2-6-2T No 6147 hurries down the gradient and into the single bore Ledbury tunnel with the 4.38pm Worcester Foregate Street to Ledbury local service on 24 June 1964. It had just entered the single line section, the track on the left being a refuge siding for runaways. Most local services were now DMU operated, but a few steam hauled peak hours ones survived including this well-used service for returning school children from Worcester to the Malvern area. BEN ASHWORTH

Ledbury Station is approached, having just emerged from the smoke filled tunnel, by Worcester's No 6848 *Toddington Grange* with the 9.15am Paddington to Hereford on 23 May 1964. The Worcester 'Grange' would have taken over from a 'Castle' at Shrub Hill for the final leg of the journey. GERALD T. ROBINSON

Shelwick Junction on the approaches to Hereford, where the line from Shrewsbury is joined. Old Oak Common's No 5014 *Goodrich Castle* eases off the curve in July 1960 with the 12.45pm Paddington to Hereford. This was one of several through Old Oak Common 'Castle' workings, although probably with a Worcester crew now in charge. The twelve years old author may well have been waiting on Hereford station to see what delights from the capital were being sent down that day. The photographer was a fellow school friend who had cycled to this out of town location. JOHN GOSS

Hereford Station. Another magnificent looking Old Oak Common 'Castle' No 5043 *Earl of Mount Edgcumbe* runs tender first along Hereford station's middle road, having just been detached from the terminated 10.03am from Oxford on 4 June 1960. This out of pattern service was withdrawn the following year when the 9.45am Paddington to Hereford was retimed thirty minutes earlier. GREAT WESTERN TRUST

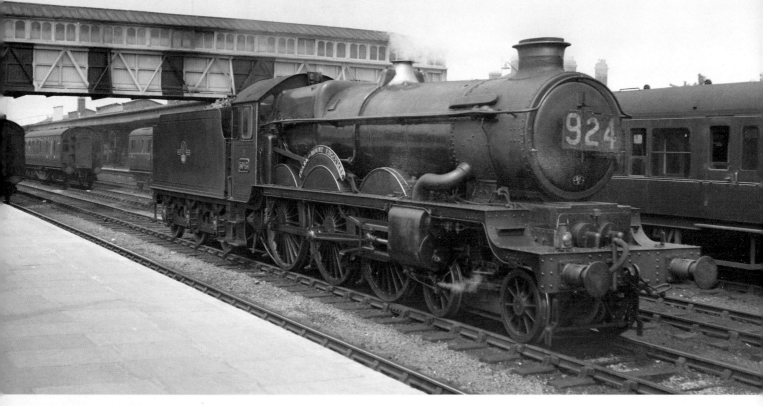

Great Malvern. Returning back up the main line towards Worcester, the depot's No 7002 *Devizes Castle* runs into Great Malvern with the 8am Hereford to Paddington 'The Cathedrals Express' on 9 May 1963. Three young smartly uniformed school children are amongst those waiting for this popular 8.42am departure towards Worcester and beyond. BEN ASHWORTH

Malvern Link. Stourbridge Junction's 4MT No 6129 makes a call here with the 6.35pm Ledbury to Worcester Foregate Street, the return working of the Worcester to Ledbury schools train, on 29 March 1965. R.N. Pritchard

Rare Visitor at Malvern Wells in c1962 is Leeds Holbeck 6P/5F 'Jubilee' 4-6-0 No 45639 *Raleigh*, having terminated in the Malvern area with a visiting excursion train. The engine, a long standing Holbeck resident from June 1951 to September 1963 withdrawal, would more usually have been seen passing through the county along the ex-Midland Railway route on a Leeds to Bristol express. Tim Farebrother

Malvern Wells. Worcester's No 6984 *Owsden Hall* shunts what appears to be an engineering train at Malvern Wells in about 1960. Worcester fireman Doug Davies is on the footplate. The Malvern Hills rising behind make a delightful backdrop to the scene. The engine had been transferred to Worcester from Hereford in June 1958 and would move on to Neyland in February 1963. TIM FAREBROTHER

Malvern Link. Gloucester Horton Road's 3F 0-6-0PT No 3616, apparently on loan to Worcester, pauses at Malvern Link with the short daily trip from Worcester to Malvern Wells on 27 July 1965. The end is nigh for all around as No 3616 would be withdrawn that September, the downside yard behind the signal box taken out of use in October and the signal box closed in December 1965. R.N. PRITCHARD

Engineering Train at Malvern Wells on Sunday 22 August 1965 with Worcester's 4MT 2-6-2T No 6147 in charge. Fireman Don Hills is on the footplate. No 6147 would be one of the last steam engines to be withdrawn from Worcester on 31 December 1965. R.N. PRITCHARD

Canal and Railway combine to make a highly visual scene as Worcester's 4MT 2-6-2T No 4113 crosses the Worcester & Birmingham canal between Foregate Street and Rainbow Hill Junction with a local freight on 28 October 1965. Just two months to go before the official end of steam working in the area and such scenes will soon be but a memory. The engine will be withdrawn just three weeks later on 18 November 1965. R.N. PRITCHARD

Empty Stock for the 4.34pm Worcester Foregate Street to Ledbury positions itself on the middle road at Shrub Hill, from where it will depart empty stock at 4.25pm on 13 July 1963. A little unusually worked by local 3F 0-6-0PT No 4680, this would have expected to have been worked by one of the depot's 4MT 2-6-2 prairie tanks. RICHARD POSTILL

Newland Halt, five miles out of Worcester, had opened in March 1929 and was now little used, with only three down calling trains per day. It and other minor halts closed on Saturday 3 April 1965. Here the penultimate service on that final day, the 4.25pm Worcester Foregate Street to Ledbury, runs into the station. This train would continue to run the following week on a faster schedule cutting journey time to Malvern by ten minutes. In charge is Stourbridge Junction's 4MT 2-6-2T No 4168. R.N. PRITCHARD

Bransford Road, three and a half miles out of Worcester, was a proper minor station located in between the 1920s opened halts leaving the city. As the ominous road in the station title suggests it was somewhat remote from the village and it too would close on 3 April 1965. Here, a Collett 4MT 2-6-2T leaves the station in around 1960 with a local passenger service from Worcester. M. HALE. GREAT WESTERN TRUST

Ledbury Station, with somewhat unusually Worcester's 4MT 2-6-2T No 4113 in charge of this four coach portion of a Hereford to Paddington service around 1960. Despite the short length of these Paddington portions as far as Worcester, they were usually entrusted to a 7P 'Castle', 5MT 'Hall' or 'Grange' 4-6-0. M. HALE. GREAT WESTERN TRUST

Midland Working. Somewhat unusually, there was for many years a daily 5.25pm Birmingham New Street to Malvern Wells, via Bromsgrove, service off the Midland route. An interesting working for local enthusiasts, it was worked by a Saltley engine; the depot turning out anything from a 5MT 'Black 5' 4-6-0 to a 6P/5F 'Crab' 2-6-0 or an underpowered 3F/4F 0-6-0. In this scene, approaching Malvern Wells in around 1961, a 4MT 2-6-0 No 43013 is the chosen steed. TIM FAREBROTHER

Worcester to Bromyard Branch

Bromyard Station. In this classic country station scene, Worcester's 3F 0-6-0PT No 4664 simmers gently as traffic is unloaded from the leading van of the 10.30am freight trip from Worcester on 24 June 1964. The guard has time to chat with the footplate crew whilst the atmospheric scene is completed by the ex-GWR gas lamp standard and a prolific display of semi-wild lupins. BEN ASHWORTH

The single track branch line from Worcester to Bromyard left the main line at Bransford Road Junction, three miles south of Worcester on the main line to Hereford. Branch passenger services started at Worcester Shrub Hill, calling at Foregate Street and on the branch at Leigh Court, Knightwick and Suckley. The minor stations on the main line after Foregate Street at Henwick, Boughton Halt and Rushwick Halt were only called at by selected branch services.

The branch had been proposed as a more ambitious Worcester-Bromyard-Leominster route, but due to financial difficulties initially only opened in October 1877 between Worcester and Bromyard. A new company was formed to complete the final section beyond there to Leominster, opening in 1884. Both sections were operated by the GWR who in 1888 purchased the line outright following the original company going into liquidation.

The through route only ever operated an infrequent passenger service, which in 1945 consisted of four services a day between Leominster and Worcester, with just three in the reverse direction. There was also an extra service each way between Worcester and Bromyard. The three 1945 balanced services from Leominster to Worcester were timed to be resourced as round trips from Leominster. The unbalanced fourth up service was a 7.45pm Leominster to Worcester. This was worked by a Worcester based ex-GWR diesel railcar returning to its home base having previously worked a Severn Valley service.

The poorly supported section between Leominster and Bromyard closed on 15 September 1952. This materially altered the resourcing pattern for remaining services between Bromyard and Worcester. Initially and until the mid-1950s this was auto-train worked by Worcester 1P 1400 0-4-2Ts. However, the last class members

Nos 1418 and 1461 were transferred away in June and October 1957 respectively. Service levels would be reduced further and by the summer 1960 timetable, this consisted of 7.43am, 5.15 and 6.50pm departures from Bromyard and only afternoon 4.10 and 5.47pm departures from Worcester. The unbalanced 7.43am Bromyard to Worcester was formed with engine and coaches off the 6am Worcester Yard to Bromyard freight and passenger empty stock. In later years, the early freight ceased to run and the first working became a straight forward passenger empty stock. Additional round trips were timetabled on Thursdays and Saturdays, when increased leisure business and shoppers supported the service. By 1960 both the 7.43am morning service and the 5.47pm round trip from Worcester were steam hauled by 5700 0-6-0PTs. The 4.10pm from Worcester round trip was worked by one of Worcester's ex-GWR diesel railcars.

The final summer 1964 timetable before closure had changed little since 1960. The early morning service and the 5.47pm from Worcester round trip were still steam hauled by a Worcester 5700 0-6-0PT. However the ex-GWR railcars had been withdrawn two years earlier and the 4.10pm from Worcester round trip was now a modern BR diesel unit.

The busiest train of the day was the 7.40am Bromyard to Worcester, conveying school children for the several independent schools there, including Alice Ottley Girls' School and Royal Grammar School Worcester. The schools traffic mostly returned on the 4.10pm, with the stragglers on the 5.47pm departure. Passenger and branch freight services were withdrawn from Monday 7 September 1964. The daily schools traffic was then conveyed by bus into and back from Worcester. One former pupil lamented, 'We liked the train because we could do our homework comfortably on the way home.'

Typical of the final years, the summer 1963 branch freight trip ran at 10.30am MWFO from Worcester Yard to Bromyard, arriving 12.11pm. A working timetable footnote added that the service had a three minutes station call at Worcester Foregate Street to pick up parcels traffic for Bromyard. It was booked to shunt at Bromyard, along with no doubt a traditional brew up for the crew, before returning at 3pm (MWFO) to Worcester Yard. By the final summer 1964 timetable, the trip was reduced to being integrated into Henwick trip and shunting duties. The freight trip now ran at 10.30am (TFO) Worcester Yard to Bromyard, with the previously

mentioned Foregate Street parcels stop, but now also performing shunting at Henwick from 10.49am to 12 noon. Bromyard was not reached until 1.15pm with, after a much reduced turnaround time, a return trip at 2.15pm (TFO) to Worcester Yard. It did not arrive there until 5.40pm having performed extended shunting duties at Henwick from 3.30 to 5.30pm. This final 1964 trip was diagrammed to be worked by a Worcester 4F 9400 0-6-0PT, but photos have not been found of this combination and it may have in practice usually been worked by the more usual 3F 5700 0-6-0PT.

Several special passenger workings over the branch are worthy of mention.

Bransford Road Junction. Worcester's 3F 0-6-0PT No 4614 passes Bransford Road Junction signal box with a brake van from the Malvern area towards Worcester in c1960. The Bromyard branch curves away to the right, the pair of tracks leading off the main line converging to a single line around the corner. M. HALE. GREAT WESTERN TRUST

Although all services had been withdrawn on the Bromyard to Leominster section in September 1952, track lifting was not threatened until 1958. A final special rail tour was organised by the Stephenson Locomotive Society from Worcester to Leominster on 26 April 1958, with photographic stops at selected stations along the officially closed final section. The service was hauled by Worcester's 4MT 4500 2-6-2T No 4571, which would be transferred to Plymouth Laira in December 1958.

On Sunday 6 September 1964, the day after the final scheduled branch service had run, a special charter train was organised from Bromyard to Blackpool hauled by a pair of Worcester 3MT 2251 0-6-0s, Nos 2222 and 2232. The latter engine was almost immediately withdrawn week ending 12 September 1964, whilst No 2222 would soldier on until May 1965 withdrawal.

Hayley Dingle Viaduct, between Leigh Court and Knightwick, is crossed by Worcester's 3F 0-6-0PT No 4664 on 24 June 1964 with the 10.30am Worcester Yard to Bromyard branch freight trip. Youthful Worcester fireman Bernard Tirebuck leans out of the cab. BEN ASHWORTH

Bromyard Station. This delightfully framed picture captures 3F 0-6-0 No 4664 on 24 June 1964 about to shunt a mineral wagon off the rear of the train's vans left on the station platform. A BR goods delivery vehicle can be seen backed up to the station front whilst the water storage tank and goods shed can be seen on the left. A semi-wild display of lupins has taken over part of the station platform. BEN ASHWORTH

An ex-GWR Diesel Railcar stands in the platform at Bromyard in this undated scene waiting for its return working to Worcester. Operation of the sparse branch service was shared between these and 3F 5700 0-6-0PT steam haulage. The goods yard is still busy with no less than ten vans in view. STEVE BARTLETT COLLECTION

Special Train Fencote. Worcester's 4MT 4500 2-6-2T No 4571 pauses at Fencote, between Bromyard and Leominster, on 26 April 1958 with a Stephenson Locomotive Society special train. Services had been withdrawn over this section in September 1952, but remarkably the track was still usable and this Worcester to Leominster special train had been arranged with track lifting imminent. DAVE WALDREN

Hayley Dingle, between Leigh Court and Knightwick, is passed through by Worcester's 3F 0-6-0PT No 8793 with the 5.45pm Worcester Shrub Hill to Bromyard on 28 July 1964. The vigorous tree growth surrounding the train on all sides adds to this delightful country scene. BEN ASHWORTH

Leaving Knightwick with its return working, the 6.50pm Bromyard to Worcester Shrub Hill, on 28 July 1964 is Worcester's 3F 0-6-0PT No 8793. Knightwick had a single platform with no passing loop. The crossover led behind the trees to a small goods siding, whilst the right hand track was a head shunt ending in a stop block. BEN ASHWORTH

Leigh Court.
A Bromyard to Worcester service makes a call headed by the usual 3F 5700 class 0-6-0PT. There was no crossing loop here and the signal box formerly controlled access to the goods siding. The signal box had closed in October 1956, replaced by a ground frame. A passenger waits for the train whilst several platform trolleys are in view apparently still seeing some use. M. HALE. GREAT WESTERN TRUST

Knightwick Station. Ex-GWR diesel railcar No W7W runs into Knightwick with a Bromyard to Worcester Shrub Hill service on Saturday 20 April 1957. Two ladies are preparing to board the train and at least its station call on this trip would prove worthwhile. W7W entered service in July 1935, delivered direct to Worcester where it spent most of its working life before withdrawal from Stourbridge Junction in January 1959. M. HALE. GREAT WESTERN TRUST

The End is Nigh as these fateful posters appear on station notice boards. They would later be supplemented by a glued strip that passenger and freight facilities would be withdrawn from Monday 7 September 1964. M. Hale. Great Western Trust

Western Region

British Railways Board

Transport Act 1962

Withdrawal of railway passenger services

The Minister of Transport has given his consent to the Board's proposal to discontinue all passenger train services between **WORCESTER (Shrub Hill)** and **BROMYARD** and from the following stations :-

LEIGH COURT
KNIGHTWICK
SUCKLEY
BROMYARD

The terms of the Minister's consent can be inspected at local booking offices

The date the services will be withdrawn will be announced later.

Main Line Freight Trains

No 7820 *Dinmore Manor*, based at Oxley, brings a freight train from the West Midlands through Worcester Shrub Hill towards Norton Junction in April 1965. There it either will drop down the chord to Abbots Wood Junction for Gloucester or continue on across the Cotswolds towards Oxford. ROGER LAMB

Long distance freight services regularly passed through the city along all three sides of the Worcester triangle. Many of these were worked by through engines from other depots and most paused in the area to be regulated for passing passenger services, locomotive watering and train crew relief. Worcester crews were heavily involved in working these forward in all directions. As footplate relief took place, pleasantries would be exchanged including from the incoming crew the state of the engine. This in the prevailing climate towards the end of steam might not always be good news. There were also some starting freight services from Worcester Yard, although these were small in number compared with the through workings. However inwards traffic was sorted here for onwards distribution using a range of exclusively steam hauled local freight trips.

Some of the long distance freight train routes mirrored those taken by passenger services, but a number wound their way across the country using routings now long forgotten in the mists of time. Routing patterns had changed little since rail nationalisation in 1948 and in this part of the world they still mainly followed former company lines or even more interestingly, exercising former long held running powers over competitors' routes. Notably passing through Worcester were services from Bristol and the West of England for Crewe, Wolverhampton and the West Midlands. These services with very much GWR origins approached Worcester via Abbotts Wood Junction having run over the ex-LMS (Midland Railway) route from Gloucester and the West. They were following what had been ex-GWR running powers over this ex-LMS (Midland Railway) route. From Bristol these services from the West of England initially followed GWR metals

via Filton Junction and Stoke Gifford before joining the ex-Midland Railway route at Yate. From there, historic GWR running powers had existed through Gloucester and on to Cheltenham. There services for the immediate Birmingham area branched right on to the GWR's own line to Birmingham via Stratford-upon-Avon. Meanwhile, others continued northwards from Cheltenham, still on the Midland Railway route as far as Abbotts Wood Junction and into Worcester. Having paused for train crew relief and locomotive watering, they continued over former GWR metals to Stourbridge Junction and into the West Midlands. At Stourbridge Junction, some services forked left towards Dudley and the now long closed link from there to Wolverhampton and Oxley yard. A few destined for Crewe still fiercely clung to former GWR metals as far as they could by being routed via Market Drayton and Nantwich until Crewe was reached. Express passenger services from Plymouth to Manchester and Liverpool however were quite differently routed from Bristol via the Severn Tunnel, Hereford and Shrewsbury to Crewe.

Another important freight artery passing through Worcester was that from South Wales to the West Midlands via Hereford. Over half of these started from Pontypool Road's large marshalling yard, whilst others originated from Llandilo Junction, Cardiff and Hereford. They were mostly destined for Stourbridge Junction, Oxley and Birmingham's Bordesley yard. They all received banking assistance up the steeply graded route under the Malvern Hills from Ledbury. These approached Worcester through Foregate Street station and took the left fork at Rainbow Hill Junction along the side of the Worcester triangle. A loop was provided on this section adjacent to the shed site where freight trains would pause for water and train crew relief. Just two each day took the right hand fork through Shrub Hill heading for Oxford's Yarnton yard.

Indeed, the line from Worcester to Oxford over the Cotswolds was another important freight artery for Oxford and London area traffic and several of these evening fast freight services started from Worcester Yard. The route included the need for assistance up the challenging Campden bank from Honeybourne. Tables listing freight trains passing through both Ledbury and Honeybourne can be found in the sub-sheds chapter.

Another long forgotten freight route, that can be identified from that list of freight services passing through Honeybourne, involved no less than seven services a day from South Wales to Yarnton yard routed via Chepstow, Gloucester and then the ex-Midland Railway route as far as Ashchurch, exercising those useful running powers yet again. From Ashchurch, they took the ex-Midland Railway route to

Evesham, where they gained the Cotswolds line through Honeybourne to the Oxford area. In 1960, these services started from Aberdare, Cardiff (2), Rogerstone (2), Llandilo Junction and Neath. For the enthusiast they brought interesting South Wales based motive power to the Cotswolds route. The Ashchurch to Evesham line closed in September 1963 and these Yarnton services were then diverted via a variety of alternative routes. This included several coming into the area via Cheltenham Malvern Road and Toddington to Honeybourne. There they had a lengthy layover whilst the through South Wales engines turned via the Honeybourne triangle before obtaining the assistance of a banking engine and on to Yarnton.

In those far off days we all understood the passenger network so well, but perhaps now realise how little some of us knew about the complex cross country freight routings that were still being taken.

No 4951 *Pendeford Hall*, a Reading based engine, steadily accelerates through Battenhall Cutting shortly after leaving Worcester with an express freight train for the London area. The date is 30 May 1958 and it will soon be passing Norton Junction where it will take the Cotswolds route towards Oxford. BRIAN PENNEY

No 6813 *Eastbury Grange.* It's Saturday 22 August 1964 and this Worcester engine and crew have just passed Standish Junction, probably heading for Bristol's Stoke Gifford yard. The service would have passed over the Gloucester Avoiding Line and crossed from the Western to the Midland route at Standish Junction. The line to Swindon and Paddington climbs away behind the train. JOHN GOSS

No 4991 *Cobham Hall,* looking in fine condition, forms up its own service at Evesham in the early 1960s. With Vale of Evesham fruit and vegetable traffic on offer in large quantities there was always much originating business to be despatched from Evesham. The small single road engine shed can be seen in the left background. F.A. HAYNES

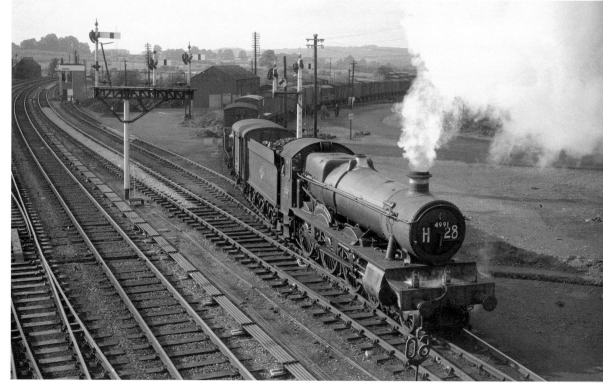

No 5322 4MT 2-6-0 of Pontypool Road, looking care worn, brings a train of South Wales coal over the Cotswolds route near Windmill Hill, between Norton Junction and Stoulton. This August 1917 built engine would become the second oldest class member still operational when continuing to earn its keep until April 1964 withdrawal. F.A. HAYNES

No 6874 *Haughton Grange* photographed from Norton Junction signal box heading for Worcester as it brings a West Midlands bound freight train off the chord line from Abbots Wood Junction and the Bristol area. F.A. HAYNES

No 6906 *Chicheley Hall* of Banbury hurries off the Cotswolds route towards Norton Junction and Worcester with a down freight. No 6906 was already a Banbury engine on 1 January 1948 and would spend its whole working life based there until April 1965 withdrawal. F.A. HAYNES

Malvern Wells between Hereford and Worcester. An unidentified Southall based Churchward 8F 2800 class 2-8-0 leisurely takes water on the up main with a freight train from South Wales in 1965. The signalman must have been confident no passenger services were due as the train could have been put into the up loop to take water. TIM FAREBROTHER

No 6946
Heatherden Hall
of Pontypool Road
working hard up
Campden Bank with
a train of South
Wales coal probably
destined for Yarnton
Yard, near Oxford. It
is early 1963 and the
snow from the bitter
1962/63 winter still
lies on the ground.
A Honeybourne
banking engine,
almost certainly a
3MT 2251 0-6-0,
will be assisting out
of view at the rear.
F.A. HAYNES

No 45253 of Saltley shed approaches Evesham with a freight train for the Oxford and London area in the early 1960s. This Black 5 4-6-0 was Saltley based between November 1959 and October 1962, helping to date the photograph. LMR motive power became increasingly common over the Cotswolds line as the 1960s progressed, partly due to route closures elsewhere leading to traffic diversions. F.A. HAYNES

No 92239 of Eastleigh climbing Campden Bank with a train of returning empty oil tanks from Bromford Bridge to Fawley in the early 1960s. Five Western Region based 9F 92000 class 2-10-0s were transferred to Eastleigh in 1961 when oil trains from Fawley to the West Midlands were diverted away from via Bristol to via Oxford and the Cotswolds line. Worcester footplate crews regularly worked these services both in steam days and after they were dieselised. F.A. HAYNES

No 48404, with steam to spare, having recently paused for water and a train crew change, emerges from Worcester Tunnel on 3 July 1965 with a freight train probably bound for Stourbridge Junction or Oxley. The engine was Shrewsbury based. The impressive signal gantry announces the three way junction on the Worcester side of the tunnel where the line will split for the goods avoiding line, Shrub Hill station or Foregate Street and the Hereford route. RALPH WARD

Rundown to Shed Closure

No 6856 *Stowe Grange* in filthy external condition, devoid of name but not number plates, at home depot Worcester on 27 March 1965. We are now in the final nine months leading up to depot closure with typically locomotive ash and discarded footplate tools littering the trackside. R.N. PRITCHARD

85A Worcester
Allocation 13 February 1965

'Hall' 5MT 4-6-0	'Grange' 5MT 4-6-0	5101 4MT 2-6-2T
5971 *Merevale Hall*	6813 *Eastbury Grange*	4113
6958 *Oxburgh Hall*	6817 *Gwenddwr Grange*	4161
Total: 2	6819 *Highnam Grange*	Total: 2
	6836 *Estevarney Grange*	
'Modified Hall' 5MT 4-6-0	6848 *Toddington Grange*	**6100 4MT 2-6-2T**
6995 *Benthall Hall*	6856 *Stowe Grange*	6147
7904 *Fountains Hall*	6877 *Llanfair Grange*	6155
7909 *Heveningham Hall*	Total: 7	6169
7919 *Runter Hall*		Total: 3
7920 *Coney Hall*	**2251 3MT 0-6-0**	
7928 *Wolf Hall*	2222	**5700 3F 0-6-0PT**
Total: 6	2244	3615
	2253	3682
	Total: 3	4664
		4680
		Total: 4
		Total Steam: 27

1965, which was the final year leading up to shed closure, would prove a difficult time for both shed and footplate staff. Locomotives were in increasingly poor condition and repairs had strict expenditure limits, with failures in traffic leading to unexpected short notice withdrawals. Replacement engines transferred in were often in little better condition and would present fresh hidden challenges for the shed maintenance staff. The depot's comparatively large 'Hall', 'Modified Hall' and 'Grange' allocation continued to cover long distance freight work and several passenger turns. Indeed the area's steam motive power despite its condition was still essential in keeping the network operational until enough diesels were available or services rationalised.

In February 1965, twenty-seven engines remained on the allocation; fifteen or well over half 'Hall', 'Modified Hall' and 'Grange' 4-6-0s. The twenty-seven engines were required to cover twenty turns daily.

The fifteen remaining 5MT 4-6-0s had thirteen daily diagrams; ten on freight work, two passenger and one spare for specials. This 5MT 4-6-0 workload required an eighty-seven per cent locomotive availability; an exceptionally challenging target given the state of much of the fleet and almost certainly not always met.

By May 1965, the large engine fleet had dipped to eleven 5MT 4-6-0s covering nine daily diagrams. Eight of these turns were on freight work and one spare for specials. Based on the depot's official monthly workload returns the scheduled passenger work disappeared at the end of April. However, what was planned did not always reflect the situation on the ground. Certainly, the diesel hauled 5.25pm Birmingham New Street to Gloucester Eastgate local passenger service continued to change engines at Worcester Shrub Hill, with a Worcester 'Hall' or 'Grange' working forward. This engine was booked to return on a Gloucester to Stourbridge Junction freight service. The summer 1965 timetable however brought a new steam turn to the depot when the 3.15pm Paddington to Worcester was extended to Hereford, with an engine change to steam at Worcester. This forward engine and its short portion returned as a 7.05pm Hereford to Worcester empty stock and parcels. As ever, anything from a Worcester 'Hall', 'Grange' or BR Standard 4MT 75000 4-6-0 might appear. The duty was dieselised in September 1965, although steam substitution still occasionally occurred.

In the final months of 1965, there was a large amount of locomotive transfer activity, as well as the inevitable withdrawals, as the Western Region struggled to keep enough serviceable steam engines available. The last 'Halls' and 'Modified Halls' were transferred away or withdrawn in July, but this was balanced by the 'Grange' allocation rising to eight engines. However around this time it was reported that the 9.45pm Worcester Yard to Pontypool Road freight, booked for a Worcester 'Grange', had been cancelled on several occasions due to no serviceable locomotive being available.

The condition of the depot's once so reliable 'Granges' was becoming a serious concern. Then the cavalry arrived in the form of six BR Standard 4MT 75000 4-6-0s made redundant from the West Country. In late May, Nos 75008, 75022 and 75025 arrived from Exmouth Junction, followed in mid-June by Nos 75000, 75003 and 75005 from Yeovil. The latter engine did not remain operational long, ending up on its side down a steep embankment at Fosse Road loop, near Leamington, on 14 September 1965 whilst working a Highworth Junction to Bordesley freight. It would never work again, although not formally withdrawn until November. The depot's eight 'Granges' struggled on

with some unserviceable until a mass cull in November 1965. Five were then withdrawn, whilst Nos 6847 *Tidmarsh Grange*, 6848 *Toddington Grange* and 6872 *Crawley Grange* were transferred to Oxford which seemed to be one of the gathering grounds for serviceable mixed traffic engines. This left just four BR Standard 4MT 75000 4-6-0s at Worcester to see out the final month's large engine requirements at Worcester.

Turning to the depot's small engines fleet in that final year, whilst four out of eleven turns had been lost at the end of December 1964, workload then stabilised. The seven turns that remained continued unchanged between January and the final surviving May 1965 monthly locomotive working return. However it is likely most turns continued well after that date. Three or four 5700 0-6-0PTs remained on the allocation during this period responsible for two daily duties. The first was the Henwick shunt and Malvern Wells freight trip. The second was a pilot turn shunting the carriage and wagon and locomotive works in the morning and covering the Shrub Hill station passenger pilot in the afternoon. Between four and five 4MT 5101/6100 2-6-2Ts remained well employed with three local freight tripping turns on the Kidderminster and Cotswolds lines. The last two 3MT 2251 0-6-0s found work covering the two daily turns on Honeybourne banking duties and associated freight trip working. When the last examples were withdrawn in May 1965, their duties, which would survive until Honeybourne's sub-shed closure at the end of the year, were covered by BR Standard 4MT 75000 4-6-0s or 4MT 5101/6100 2-6-2Ts.

Worcester steam shed would close with effect from Monday 3 January 1966, although the depot's last nine engines were formally withdrawn on Friday 31 December 1965.

85A Worcester – Final Steam Allocation
All Withdrawn 31 December 1965

75000 4MT 4-6-0	5700 3F 0-6-0PT
75000	3682
75008	4680
75022	9626
75025	
	Total: 9
6100 4MT 2-6-2T	
6147	
6165	

Worcester Shed. The Passenger Shed on the left and the Goods shed to the right on 31 July 1965. All the signs are that the end is near with withdrawn and out of steam engines lined up. In the foreground in steam are Oxford's No 7909 *Heveningham Hall* and 'minus number and number plates but still operational' Tyseley's No 6854 *Roundhill Grange*. RALPH WARD

No 75005 outside Worcester's Goods Shed on 21 August 1965. It was one of six BR Standard 4MT 4-6-0s that arrived in May/June 1965 to assist the ailing 5MT 'Grange' 4-6-0s. No 75005 would end up on its side down an embankment at Fosse Road loop whilst hauling a freight train on 14 September 1965 and never worked again. RALPH WARD

Worcester Shed. In an atmospheric scene on 20 November 1965, an unidentified BR Standard 4MT 75000 4-6-0 simmers quietly in the Goods shed. It is just over a month to depot closure and soon such scenes will be no more. RALPH WARD

No 5971 *Merevale Hall* in poor external condition with cab side number plate missing and light steam gently wisping from several places away whilst on shed in June/July 1965. This was near the end of the engine's final spell at Worcester from 26 December 1964 until a 17 July 1965 transfer to Bristol Barrow Road. Worcester's No 7904 *Fountains Hall* was transferred at the same time, ending the class's association with Worcester. A born survivor, *Merevale Hall* would be spared Bristol Barrow Road's November 1965 shed closure, moving on again to Oxford where it would be withdrawn in the final December 1965 Western Region mass steam cull. DEREK SHORT. PETE SKELTON COLLECTION

Nameplate removal for safe keeping and sale is about to take place on the same day as the previous photograph by Worcester fireman Peter Hull and driver Jeff Hocking. DEREK SHORT. PETE SKELTON COLLECTION

Merevale Hall's nameplate removed is displayed by Worcester driver Jeff Hocking and fireman Peter Hull, screwdriver in hand. I would have thought the task was really a fitter's job, but then Worcester crews were a multi-tasking lot. The nameplate is believed to have been purchased by the locally based photographer. DEREK SHORT. PETE SKELTON COLLECTION

Worcester Shed three months after shed closure on 31 March 1966. An end wall now seals the back of the Passenger Shed, on the right, which is being converted to a diesel servicing depot. Shunting engines will be based there whilst main line engines will also be fuelled and serviced. Condemned steam engines still await their fate in the background. R.N. PRITCHARD

Appendices

Worcester Allocated Engines – Photograph Index

Locomotive	Page Number	Locomotive	Page Number
6877	58	8106	70
		8107	71
6947	55		
6984	189	8415	76
6992	23, 53		
		8793	199, 200
7000	106		
7002	106, 120, 187	9429	141
7004	49, 107, 118, 174		
7005	21, 26, 107, 108, 115, 119, 121	75000	59
7006	109	75003	60
7007	39, 90, 94, 109, 110, 115, 145	75005	215
7009	126	75022	60
7011	34, 35, 111, 125		
7013	20, 112, 119	78001	72, 143, 147
7022	112	78008	156
7023	36, 37, 92, 113, 117, 142, 181		
7025	20, 21, 38, 113, 116, 117, 175	82030	71
7027	38, 118, 122		
7031	24, 40, 122	W6W	131
		W7W	201
7750	141	W20W	134
		W22W	131, 172
7920	53	W26W	135, 136
7928	11, 54, 124	W32W	132, 132

Worcester Named Footplate and Shed Staff – Photograph Index

Name	Page Number	Name	Page Number
District Management		Jack Saunders	35
George Bartlett	30	Chris Smith	34
Guy Kerry	141	Bernard Tirebuck	197
		Jeff Yates	35
Shed Masters			
Fred Cole	30		**Chargeman Cleaner**
Harry Cureton	28	Fred Jones	34, 36
Drivers			**Maintenance Foreman**
Ken Alford*	35	Don Green	91, 141
Reg Dancox*	36		
Sid Haynes	37		**Maintenance Staff**
Jeff Hocking	216, 217	Ron Ashby	91
Neville Hodson	75	Richard Giblett	91
Charlie Huntley	55	Ernie Payne	91
Peter Jackson	26, 38	Frank Waters	24, 34, 108
Len Long	39		
Sidney Page	155		**Shed Clerical Staff**
Bill Shuard	39	Alan Barber	30
Tommy Smith	74	Joe Bridgwater	30
Allen Tapper	39	Harry Collins	30
Jim Teal	39	Steve James	30
Geoff Truby	40	Hugh Lamour	30
	* Acting Shed Running Foremen	Ben Lewis	30
Firemen/Cleaners		Bill Shepherd	30
Bill Adams	75	John Summers	30
Roy Cale	38	Peter Westwood	30
Alan Collins	34		
Dougie Davies	40, 189		**Guards**
Mick Fenson	77	Bill Garrett	155
Doug Hatton	39	Arthur Savage	39
Ron Harris	35		
Rob Hemming	34		
Don Hills	190		
Brian Hodson	75		
Brian Houseman	37		
Ray Hughes	155		
Peter Hull	216, 217		
Peter Kitson	35		
Tim O'Grady	40		
Brian Parsons	34		
Mick Rock	36		
George Robbins	35		

Bibliography

COOKE R.A., *Track Layout Diagrams of the GWR and BRWR – No 28 Worcester-Oxford Line and Branches*, 1976

COOKE R.A., *Track Layout Diagrams of the GWR and BRWR – No 33 Worcestershire*, 1976

JUDGE Colin, *The History of the Great Western A.E.C. Diesel Railcars*, Noodle Books 2008

KENNEDY Rex, *Steam on the Great Western: Severn & Cotswolds*, Ian Allan Publishing 1993

LONGWORTH Hugh, *BR Steam Locomotives Complete Allocations History 1948-1968*, OPC (an input of Ian Allan Publications) 2014

LYONS E., *An Historical Survey of Great Western Engine Sheds*, Oxford Publishing Co. 1974

Records and Journals

'BR–WR Engine Record Cards AN7/116-126', National Archives, Kew

'BR–WR Engine Diagram Summary by Shed 1963-65 AN7/85-87', National Archives Kew

Great Western Railway Journal No 84 'Worcester Locomotive Works' by Brian Penney and Richard Parker

Great Western Railway Journal Nos 93-95 'Worcester Running Shed' by Brian Penney and Richard Parker

'BR-WR Working Timetables', Various 1960-1966

Trains Illustrated/Modern Railways, Monthly 1960-1966

'Railway Locomotives', *British Locomotive Society Journal Monthly* 1960-66

'The Railway Observer', *Railway Correspondence and Travel Society Journal* 1961-1965